The Crisis

in Black and Black

Earl Ofari Hutchinson, Ph.D.

Also by Earl Ofari Hutchinson

The Myth of Black Capitalism
Let Your Motto Be Resistance
The Mugging of Black America
Black Fatherhood: The Guide to Male Parenting
Black Fatherhood II: Black Women Talk About Their Men
The Assassination of the Black Male Image
Beyond O.J.: Race, Sex, and Class Lessons for America
Blacks and Reds: Race and Class in Conflict, 1919-1990
Betrayed: Presidential Failure to Protect Black Lives

The Crisis
in Black and Black

by
Earl Ofari Hutchinson, Ph.D.

Middle Passage Press

Middle Passage Press
5517 Secrest Drive
Los Angeles, CA 90043

Publisher's Cataloging-in-Publication
(Provided by Quality Books, Inc.)

Hutchinson, Earl Ofari.
    The crisis in black and black / Earl Ofari Hutchinson. —
1st ed.
    p. cm.
    Includes bibliographical references and index.
    ISBN: 1-881032-14-0 (hbk.)
    ISNB: 1-881032-15-9 (pbk.)

    1. Afro-Americans—Social conditions. 2. Social conflict
—United States. 3. Afro-Americans—Race identity. I. Title.

    E185.86.H88 1998   305.8'96073
                             98-65095

Dedication

To my grandmothers who taught me to think for myself and to be myself.

Acknowledgements

Special thanks to Matt Blair, Joye Day, and Rene Childress. They proved that no writer can succeed without the support and encouragement of those who care. Also a special thanks to my publisher, Barbara Bramwell, for her committment and support in publishing some of my works.

Contents

Foreword

With his previous books and essays, Earl Ofari Hutchinson has established himself as one of the most thoughtful, provocative and courageous thinkers on the American scene. He has proven himself to be a writer of wit and style whose insights are well worth the price of admission.

With *The Crisis in Black and Black*, Hutchinson takes another giant literary step forward and provides a worthy follow-up to Charles Silberman's *The Crisis in Black and White*, first published more than a quarter of a century ago. Hutchinson wades into a host of controversial subjects, exploring everything from black ambivalence about Louis Farrakhan to the foolishness of rallying behind O.J. Simpson; and he does so fearlessly.

If you have not yet discovered Hutchinson, you owe it to yourself to do so.

Ellis Cose, Editor, *Newsweek*
Author of *The Rage of a Privileged
Class* and *Color-Blind: Seeing Beyond
Race in a Race Obsessed World*

OUR OWN WORST ENEMY— AN OVERVIEW

The biggest twist in black-white relations in the last decade of the Twentieth Century is that the issue of racism which divides blacks and whites has been nearly overtaken by an imploding crisis that divides many African-Americans apart from one another. How has the ancient crisis in black and white now become the modern-day crisis in black and black?

I was in college when I first read Charles Silberman's landmark work, *The Crisis in Black and White*.[1] That was in the late 1960s. The title was more than appropriate at that time. America's cities were burning, the civil rights movement was cresting; Malcolm X and Dr. Martin Luther King, Jr. had been murdered; and blacks were shouting "Black Power" and "pick up the gun." The FBI's secret plot to smash the black power movement was in full swing. President Richard Nixon and many conservatives were screaming for law and order, and denouncing crime in the streets, and permissiveness—universally interpreted by political insiders to mean the excesses and lawlessness of blacks. This firmly planted the seeds of the conservative revolt that budded on the surface during the White House tenure of Ronald Reagan in the 1980s and exploded from the surface in the 1990s in the pillage of affirmative action and the meat ax of social programs.

It seemed that blacks and whites were locked in a bitter dance of hostility and conflict; in short, a crisis in black and white. In a perverse sense, that made things so much simpler for many blacks and for whites. They could comfortably view America through race colored lenses. This allowed many blacks to rail against the "white man," "white power structure," or "the white establishment" and delude themselves that America teetered dangerously on the brink of a coming apocalyptic race war.

This same delusion struck many whites and launched them on the most riotous and reckless domestic weapons spending spree in this country's history. In the process, it laid the seed for the massive police-prosecutor-prison-industrial complex that has sprung full blown in the 1990s.

In the quarter century since *The Crisis in Black and White* was published, much has changed. The crisis in race relations has taken many odd twists and turns. Perhaps the biggest twist is that the issue of race and racism which divides blacks and whites has been nearly overshadowed by an imploding crisis that divides many African-Americans apart from one another.

The changing racial dynamic of the past decade is now marked by schism and conflict between the black middle class and the poor, black women and men; the black intellectual elite and the black rappers and gang leaders; black politicians and the politically alienated black urban poor; and, black conservatives and black liberal/radicals.

It has generated differing reactions to racism, affirmative action; the commercial exploitation and reinforcement of stereotypes by some black filmmakers, rappers, and comedians; gender attacks by some black feminists on black men; self-destructive violence by some young black males and females; a profound leadership gap; and, conspiracy paranoia. These issues are incessantly discussed and hotly debated within and without the black communities.

A quarter century ago, few in their most outlandish dreams would have thought that someday they would hear and see:

• A black U.S. Supreme Court justice, appointed by a conservative Republican president, trounce affirmative action, abortion, and civil liberties; vote to dilute black political strength; vote to end school busing; and vote to wildly expand police power—while some blacks cheer him for doing it.

• Blacks, in a militant march of a million or more blacks on Washington, flog themselves for drugs, crime, absence of family values, father absenteeism, and failure to vote; in other words, call for a return to good, old Americana values.

• A legion of black sports stars rake in king's ransom salaries and monster-sized commercial endorsement deals while being accused by many blacks of abandoning the black community and promoting the delusion that sports is the only ticket out of the ghetto for young blacks.

3

- Blacks spin uproarious tales in which they blame every ill, crime in the black community, and the assassination of every black leader on sinister plots and conspiracies.

- One of America's most beloved sports figures on trial for the murder of two people who were white, and many blacks batter him for being a race traitor.

- Black leaders and politicians cling to a near mystical faith in the Democratic party.

- Many middle-class blacks gleefully flee their own neighborhoods, not only because they have an opportunity to live in integrated neighborhoods, but, also because of their thinly disguised fear that black neighborhoods are no longer safe.

- Many blacks construct fantastic theories of history that virtually ignore or deny the rich contributions of blacks to American society.

- Young blacks slaughter other young blacks in numbers that exceed the death toll at the peak year of fighting of the Vietnam war.

- Black filmmakers pawn off vicious racial stereotypes, degenerate sexual escapades, Amos n' Andy buffoonery, and the "gangsta" lifestyle on the film screen as the only reality of black life.

- Many blacks gratify themselves by name-calling and bullying any black that does not adhere to a prescribed, black party-line on militancy.

- Blacks uphold as a badge of pride that most, many, or even all blacks grow up in dope-plagued, roach-ridden, rat-infested, gang-ruled, poverty-choked, fatherless ghettos where death and decay lurk at every turn.

4

• Blacks claim that they speak a distinct language other than English, demand special curricula and monies to teach it, badger other blacks who criticize them for doing it, and without a moment's hesitation would instantly call any white a "racist" who would dare do the same.

• Some black academics weave pop theories about race into instant bestsellers, bag rich honorariums, and become instant TV talk show celebrities while abandoning scholarship.

• Black women and men spend many waking hours obsessed with the notion that many, most, or all black men want white women.

• Prominent local and national black leaders crusade against gay rights—and many blacks applaud them for doing it.

• Many blacks refuse to face the naked truth that blacks are just as much if not more American than white Americans.

Who could have foreseen any of this a quarter century ago? Because these events frighteningly have come to pass, they are cautionary and prophetic warnings that the crisis in black and white of a quarter century ago has been matched and in some ways replaced today by a crisis in black and black which has turned many blacks into their own worst enemies.

A Final Comment: I know it is peculiar to start a book with a caveat. But I must warn myself and the reader to always resist the temptation to over generalize on the point that blacks are their own worst enemy. Many are not. They devote their time, energy, and resources to working for and helping other blacks and non-blacks. They are the best friends of African-Americans and among the best of the hopes for America.◆

I BELIEVE IN AMERICA: UNDERSTANDING A CLARENCE THOMAS

Black conservatives have been damned and denounced, praised and promoted, but they cannot be
ignored. For better or worse, they have always been a
part of black life. Who are they? What do they really
stand for? Are they helping or hurting the black
communities? Will more blacks call themselves conservatives in the future?

I wondered why so many blacks got teed off at NAACP
executive director, Kweisi Mfume, when in February
1997, he said that blacks should stop ganging up on
Supreme Court Justice, Clarence Thomas. Mfume called it a
waste of valuable time and energy trying to change his views.

Worse, it has made Thomas even worse. He was simply beyond hope, Mfume felt.[1]

Many blacks do not buy this. They have clamped hard onto their anti-Thomas crusade for two reasons: (1) he is the swing vote in 5-4 court decisions; and (2) he is black. Therefore, he should have some in-born sympathy to black causes. Both are questionable assumptions. Thomas has provided the fifth vote in many of the Court's most abominable decisions that decimated affirmative action, gutted civil liberties, erased minority political redistricting, and grossly broadened police power.

The same could be said for justices William Rehnquist, Anton Scalia, William Kennedy, and Sandra Day O'Conner. All four, like Thomas, were appointed by conservative Republican presidents. All four share the same strict constructionist reading of the Constitution, and range from politically conservative to right-wing retrograde in their philosophies. The only reason to separate Thomas from this bunch and expect something different from him brings me to point (2). He is black.

Mfume, I, and Thomas are African-Americans. But, that is where the resemblance ends. We are at polar opposites politically from Thomas's mummified political views. Mfume and I also know that there are packs of black politicians, talk show hosts, and writers who, for ratings, dollars, glory, and opportunism, have no compunction about saying: Find me a better country than America.

Mfume, however, did not go far enough in explaining

Thomas. I also know that when Thomas once said: "I emphasize self-help as opposed to racial quotas and race-conscious legal devices," black and white liberals were outraged. However, in 1899, another black leader used even harsher words. He called Negro homes, "breeders of idleness" and insisted that "work, continuous work must be impressed on Negro children as the road to salvation."[2]

The words were those of W.E.B. DuBois. The radical educator and political activist could hardly be mistaken for a black conservative. Yet his passionate defense of self-help and economic independence shows that despite centuries of racial oppression in America there has always been a hidden side of black thought that is less radical and more conservative than it appears at first glance. And it is that hidden conservatism among blacks that indicates how badly the debate over Thomas has gone awry.

Mainstream black leaders and liberals regard black conservatives as sideshow freaks or dangerous political Trojan horses. *Emerge* magazine, in two cover features on Thomas in 1994 and in 1996, accurately depicted his cave man political views and judicial opinions, yet still managed to plumb the depths of magazine tastelessness by depicting him on one cover as wearing a bandanna (symbolizing an Uncle Tom) while on the other cover as a grotesque grinning lawn jockey (also symbolizing an Uncle Tom).

They forgot one thing. If a white publication had dared to depict any black that way, including I suspect Thomas, they would be the first to sound the battle cry and stamp that publication with the big "R" (as in racist) word. For blacks to depict any black that way, no matter how despicable their views are considered, fans the same vile racist stereotypes that blacks have spent lifetimes trying to shed and sends the silent signal that it's okay for others to graphically mug blacks, too. Then it becomes only a short and very easy step from blacks caricaturing Thomas (who many love to hate) to whites doing the same to any African-American whom they may love to hate.

As silly as these depictions of Thomas were, there is something else that many blacks miss in the stampede to get Thomas. On the eve of the Thomas nomination confirmation hearings in 1991, a USA Today poll, found that a large number of blacks were pro-life, pro-school prayer, and anti-gun control. Forty-seven percent of blacks agreed with Thomas that self-help, not quotas, should be the goal of blacks. Some blacks poohed-poohed this then and now. They say that this is misleading, blacks are conservative on crime (more on this later) but not on social and political issues. This is just as misleading.[3]

Five years after Thomas was confirmed, black opinion showed a trend on some social issues even more to the political right than ever. Thirty percent of blacks called themselves conservatives; forty-eight percent of blacks blamed themselves, not racism, for not taking full advantage of opportunities; fifty percent favored the cutting off of welfare; and a whopping seventy-five percent backed a constitutional amendment permitting school prayer.

It would be very interesting to see what an updated opinion survey in 1998 of black attitudes toward the women's and the gay movement would turn up. The only one on black attitudes toward gays was taken several years ago and it showed that many blacks are no less, and in far too many cases, more homophobic than many whites. Much more on this later, too.[4]

There was no guesswork, however, about what blacks said when asked in 1994, "What is the main problem facing the country today?" They ranked racism next to dead last in a list of six problems. Crime and drugs were their runaway worries.

The Congressional Black Caucus, which has been virtually the last group standing for liberalism in American politics in the 1990s, seemed to have huge second thoughts about not only where much of America is politically, but where many blacks are, too. In 1997, it shifted its agenda and publicly announced that it was hitting hard on crime and drugs, and it was going to work more closely with Republicans. This was political pragmatism to the *nth* degree. It did not mean that working with the Republicans meant that they would become Republicans. It did mean that, as one put it, "they were listening to their constituents and would be on top of their beliefs."[5]

As for politics, more blacks are not in the Republican Party, not because they are inherently liberal, natural born rebels or cradle-born Democrats, but because the Republican party works round the clock to keep them out, (more on this later, too).

◆ ◆ ◆ ◆ ◆

Anyone who is even a step before comatose and has paid any attention to what many blacks say and do should not be shocked by any of this. The truth, to repeat, is that conservative values and goals have been soundly enshrined in African-American life for generations. The problem is that most white Americans never recognized this and many blacks denied it. They created a self-made myth of black liberalism. The myth largely grew out of the New Deal years of the 1930s when blacks abandoned their traditional Republican loyalties and became a key cog in the liberal-labor-ethnic coalition built by Franklin Roosevelt and the Democrats.[6]

For the next half century, blacks were staunch Democratic devotees. Soon, the public became accustomed to regarding blacks as the biggest disciples of federal spending on welfare, education, jobs, and social programs. During the late 1960s, mass civil rights demonstrations, protests, black power takeovers, and the urban uprisings turned the myth of black liberalism into the myth of black radicalism. Many Americans still firmly believe that blacks are permanent rebels out to subvert the nation's values and institutions.

These myths do not square with the past. In 1848, abolitionist leader Frederick Douglass asked: "What are the colored people doing for themselves?" Douglass was not a conservative. Yet his question and the sentiments that were behind it showed that self-help in that day were not dirty words among radical abolitionists and that in their battle for

12

freedom they were always mindful of traditional American values.[7]

Like most black leaders, Douglass challenged blacks to initiate more self-improvement programs. Throughout the Nineteenth Century, black leaders, of varied political views, from Booker T. Washington to T. Thomas Fortune, talked as much about self-help, family values, crime, and patriotism as they did about segregation and poverty. The names of black leaders—no matter what their political label—in this century who have declared that blacks are "American" and "loyal" would fill several pages.[8]

Why would they not be? African-Americans are among America's oldest native sons and daughters. They have been molded and shaped by American ideals. For the past century, black churches, social organizations, political and economic associations have generally advocated conservative programs of self-help and legal protest. The rural Southern tradition from which most blacks have emerged placed a high premium on business, church, and family relations. If not for the great stumbling blocks of racism and economic exclusion, blacks gladly would have scurried down the same path to assimilation as the European immigrants.

The Communists and Socialists quickly discovered these stumbling blocks. In some instances they helped blacks fight against them. In other instances they tried to exploit them for their own advantage. Whatever their motive, it did not work. The majority of blacks resisted the overtures from Communists and radicals, even during the Great Depression of the 1930s. When the NAACP's *Crisis* magazine in 1931 asked

13

six black newspaper editors what they thought about Communism, only one editor saw any future for it among blacks. The others were unanimous that Communism was no cure for black oppression because "of the peculiar love which Negroes have for America and American institutions." Most blacks also shunned the Socialist Party and Henry Wallace's Progressive Party in the 1930s and 1940s, even though both strongly opposed segregation and economic inequality.[9]

Influential blacks, such as newspaperman George Schuyler and trade unionist A. Phillip Randolph, actively opposed the Communists throughout the 1920s and 1930s. Schuyler's editorials and columns in the *Pittsburgh Courier* were read and endorsed by thousands of blacks nationwide. Schuyler, in his autobiography, *Black and Conservative*, published in 1966, anticipated Clarence Thomas and the black conservatives of the 1990s. He made strong appeals for self-help, business initiative, and Americanism.[10]

During America's wars, black protest quickly gave way to black patriotism. Black divisions distinguished themselves in the Civil War and the Spanish American War. At the outbreak of America's entrance into World War I, DuBois, in a *Crisis* editorial, rallied blacks to the flag with a call to "Close our Ranks" and "forget our special grievances." Loyalist fever among blacks soared during World War II. Black newspapers carried headlines "Buy a Liberty Bond and Win the War." Not only did blacks buy millions of dollars in war bonds, they also staged victory balls, rallies, and fund drives.[11]

During the Korean conflict, blacks again dutifully trudged off to yet another foreign battlefield. The massive protests and urban uprisings that tore apart America's cities during the 1960s did not dissuade blacks from fighting and dying in disproportionate numbers in Vietnam. In the Persian Gulf war in 1991, blacks composed more than one-third of the fighting force.

Even hyper-radical black protest has proved more a strange blend of media illusion, street tough talk, militant sounding phrase mongering, and political pragmatism than a permanent bellwether of changing reality. While Malcolm X blistered white America for "its racist savagery," he also made it clear in his speeches that black empowerment would come through the vote not the gun. There was little to distinguish the program of his group, The Organization of Afro-American Unity—job and skill training, business expansion, political clubs, and veterans assistance—from that of the NAACP or Urban League.[12]

Strip away the black Muslim's "the white man as devil" and the Black Panthers "pick up the gun" rhetoric in the 1960s and the Muslim's programs for farm and business development and the Panther's community breakfast and tutoring programs would then look suspiciously like the self-help programs advocated by black conservatives. One item of proof: future Supreme Court nominee Thomas certainly had no trouble telling the public in 1983 that he "admired" Louis Farrakhan's "self-help philosophy."[13]

Privately, he probably said the same again in 1997, when it was revealed that Farrakhan met with conservative Republicans at a closed door meeting in Florida to discuss "common concerns."[14]

15

At the Black Power Conference held in Newark in 1967, black militants harangued the Democrats for their "plantation politics." However, in their final political resolutions, the delegates meekly called for the election of "twelve more black congressmen" and a "recall election" to oust Newark's mayor. The National Black Political Convention in 1972 and Jesse Jackson's Rainbow Coalition movement in 1984 and 1988 never seriously considered breaking with the Democratic party. Each time their aim was to gain more leverage and representation for blacks within the Party's hierarchy. By 1996, Jackson, despite occasional outbursts of militant media rhetoric, was more snugly than ever ensconced in the bosom of the Democratic party.[15]

Most blacks have always viewed their fight for jobs, housing, education, equal opportunity, and political empowerment as part of the American democratic tradition. Even at the Million Man March in 1995 more blacks self-identified themselves as "conservatives" than "black nationalists." Blacks direct their anger at the system not because they want to destroy it but to be included in it. Take Thomas. He is as good an example as any. During his student days he paraded around the campus of Holy Cross College wearing a black leather jacket and black beret. Somewhere during his years at Yale he shed his Panther attire. And the instant he caught the drift that there was much mileage to be gained in conservative politics he dashed down the course that would move him into the fast track of business and politics. He was hardly the exception. Thousands of other "black militants" did the same when they got their piece of the action.

Critics also fire way past the mark when they assume that Thomas and other latter day black conservatives owe their political existence to Republican Party patronage. While the Republicans joyfully cultivate and promote them they did not create them.

Despite the three decades-long cold shoulder Republicans have given blacks, many have never completely closed the door to them. Republican notable Colin Powell gave not a fig of a thought to making a bid for the Democratic presidential nomination in 1996, or running as an independent candidate. Polls taken during the presidential campaign showed that 25 to 45 percent of blacks called themselves conservative.[16]

If Republican big-wigs had slithered even a fraction of an inch out from under the near death grip of the assorted Christian fundamentalist-aligned factions that boss them around and made any kind of real overture to blacks in the 1990s, the number of blacks who would have rushed to them would have caused their ranks to swell.

Even when the Republican top-cats do not budge, many blacks still back the Republican party. How many? In 1994, the worst year of Pat Buchananism-Newt Gingrichism among Republicans, twenty-three black Republicans ran for Congress; two black Republicans won state-wide offices in Colorado and Ohio; six white Republican governors won office with significant black votes; and one black state representative switched from the Democrats to the Republicans claiming that the Republicans are closer to her constituent's views on social issues than the Democrats.[17]

17

◆ ◆ ◆ ◆ ◆

There is no mystery why more blacks than many people think or admit, eyeball the Republicans and call themselves conservative. They reflect the economic blossoming of the black middle-class during the 1970s, 1980s, and 1990s. By 1994, 40 percent of black high school graduates were attending college, 64 percent of blacks owned homes, and 27.2 percent of black families earned more than $25,000 annually. In 1997, Black Enterprise *magazine reported that the top 100 black businesses had nearly $14 billion in sales. Although the wealth of the new black bourgeoisie still paled beside that of their white counterparts, the fact is that thousands of African-Americans were coming closer than ever to realizing the American Dream.*[17]

This was painful and embarrassingly apparent in California in 1996 when conservative Republicans dumped the Proposition 209 initiative on the ballot, the so-called California Civil Rights Initiative that barred affirmative action in all state programs. Almost unnoticed in the ballyhoo over the Initiative's passage was the fact that slightly more than one out of four blacks voted for it.[18]

Many tried to explain this away by saying that the blacks who supported the Initiative were confused by its deceptive language or were misled by Republican trickery. This was wishful thinking. The plain truth is that many blacks voted for it because they supported it. They were convinced that they had achieved their success in business and the professions through hard work, education, and ability. They agreed with many whites and other non-blacks that affirmative action, like welfare, discourages incentive and unfairly stigmatizes blacks as social and moral paupers eternally seeking government hand-outs. They felt insulted that many whites claimed they get ahead because of their color and not their competence.

Many younger blacks did not experience Jim Crow laws, have almost no knowledge of the civil rights battles of the 1960s that erased them, and only the fuzziest idea of how affirmative action benefits them. This deepens their feeling that affirmative action laws have little relevance to them, or aids and abets white females, Latinos and Asians more than blacks.

There is one other major issue that is often muddled with mythology within and without the black communities: Crime. Much of the public, black and non-black, still think that blacks are softer on crime than whites. They are not. The overwhelming majority of blacks favor stiffer sentences for drug use, violent crimes, and three strike laws. A scant majority now say they support the death penalty.[19]

A defense attorney with whom I am acquainted found the latter out the hard way. He told me that he would do anything to get as many blacks as possible on the jury in a murder case involving his black client. He reasoned that they were more likely to vote for acquittal. He partly got his wish when a predominantly black jury was seated. He did not get the other half of his wish. The jury convicted his client and recommended the death penalty.

He believed the fable that blacks are more sympathetic to black lawbreakers. But why should they be? The victims of black crime are almost always other blacks. Their hardened attitudes toward crime and in support of the death penalty, tougher drug and three strikes laws reflect this fear.

The call by many blacks for moral crusades against violence, more personal and family responsibility, more gang sweeps, more drug arrests, and evictions of lawbreakers from public housing, reflect not only their fear of crime but their sense that they too have a big stake in protecting their lives, property, and their hard earned valuables from criminals, including black criminals. This is ignored by many blacks and whites who perpetuate the myth that blacks are by nature more liberal or even radical than whites on all social issues.

Thomas is not an abnormality. Whether one likes his views or not, and there is a world of reasons not to, they form a secret part of the black experience. He made many Americans realize that there are millions of African-Americans who do not think that self-initiative, safe neighborhoods, and the pursuit of wealth are the sole preserves of the white middle class.

That is why when *Black Enterprise* pollsters asked blacks in 1991 if "their hopes and aspirations were the same as the white middle class," 61 percent said "yes." And in what some might consider the final irony, poor blacks, the group that the experts assure us have absolutely no more economic or political ground to lose in America, still tightly clutched to an almost school child's faith in the belief that their lot can and will improve in America. This is not to ridicule or demean blacks, poor, or otherwise, who zealously clutch to their hopes and dreams of a better life. It is to say that they believe in America, too. Understanding why they and other blacks do is to understand a Clarence Thomas.[20]

A Final Comment: Mfume was not cheerleading Thomas or black conservatism. He merely understood him and what he represented. He recognized that men and women like him were, and always have been, a fact of black life. The rise of the Thomasites merely points to the appearance of a segment of black America that has previously been invisible: a segment that did not fit the one-dimensional political image of blacks. How much real power or influence within black communities they have or will have is problematic. What is not problematic is that the national media and political leaders have taken to them with a passion and will do everything in their power to make sure the world knows they exist.

This is why the better and smarter move for the vociferous black anti-Thomasites is to storm the barricades *for* the social issues they believe in rather than storming the barricades *against* what the black conservatives believe in, especially since many other blacks believe the same thing.◆

2

Rethinking the Million Man March

Depending on who one talks to, the Million Man March was a marvelous success or a towering disappointment. What went right? What went wrong? Can or should the March happen again?

I thought Nation of Islam leader Louis Farrakhan hedged his bets in October 1996, the year after the Million Man March, when he again called the faithful together in a World Day of Atonement rally at the United Nations. To avoid the inevitable comparison to the Million Man March and to blunt potential criticism, Farrakhan shrewdly downplayed race and ideology. That raises the real question, "What has changed since the Million Man March?"[1]

It is hardly a surprise that Farrakhan still ranks highest on white America's most obnoxious list. Farrakhan, however, risked squandering the goodwill of many blacks who praised and admired him after the March by visiting Nigeria, Sudan, Lybia, Syria, Iran, and Iraq in January 1996. These are countries whose leader's deplorable human rights records are well-documented and who routinely jail, torture, and murder dissidents.

As bad as that looked, I can not let it go at that. Much of the media almost certainly distorted a lot of what Farrakhan did and said during his nineteen country visit. He probably did make a scattering of intemperate and ill-timed remarks about the racial policies of the United States government. For the most part it appeared that he confined his tour to making the rounds of ceremonial banquets, prayer rallies, courtesy visits, and photo-op sessions with the heads of state and assorted dignitaries. His speeches appeared to be calculated to be restricted to discussing biblical and spiritual themes.

His visit to the Sudan was a good example of how his appearances can be both deceptive and distorted. While he got deserved heat from some black reporters for remaining virtually closed-mouthed on the issue of slavery in the Sudan, he managed a bit of veiled criticism of that country's policies when he warned the Sudan's president that the sanctions against his country would end only when he "keeps the word of God." As always Farrakhan walked a tight line and was careful not to say or do anything to land him in a court docket back home. In 1998, Farrakhan quietly repeated his globetrotting performance. This time he visited 52 nations. I say quietly because as with most second acts: the press, the public, and the government officials (at least publicly anyway) this time mostly ignored him.[2]

Meanwhile, back in the USA, many of Farrakhan's most flaming backers were willing to ignore or excuse the actions of the dictators that run these countries. They were hard pressed to explain how Farrakhan's visited aids the battle for civil rights, affirmative action, more health, education, jobs programs, criminal justice reform, or how they would reverse the pestilence of drugs, guns, gangs and crime in black communities?

If Farrakhan, luxuriating in the afterglow of the Million Man March, saw himself as black America's main man nationally and internationally, then he had a special responsibility to carefully consider the repercussions his words and actions had on blacks. It is a baby step from painting Farrakhan as an anti-Semite, racist, and hate monger to painting blacks with the same broad brush. This would give many conservatives yet another excuse—not that they need it—to further ravage civil rights gains and social programs. This is a point that must not be side-stepped.

Images are critically important. Non-blacks, and yes, many blacks themselves, must be repeatedly reminded that the overwhelming majority of young blacks fit absolutely none of the media stereotypes of them as congenital car jackers, drive by shooters, gangbangers, dope dealers, jail fodder, and irresponsible derelicts. Yet, the crisis issues that hammer the black communities and drove thousands of black men and women to the Million Man March in Washington D.C. in October 1995 are pressing. One out of three young black males is now in prison, on probation and parole. Murder is still the number one cause of death among young black males.[3]

The gangland style murder of rappers Tupac Shakur, one month before the first year anniversary of the Million Man March, and the murder of Notorious B.I.G., five months after the first year anniversary of the March, by other blacks, was destructive proof that far too many young blacks are still hopelessly gripped by the "gangsta lifestyle." Even more shameful and disgraceful, some of those arrested for the wave of arson attacks on black churches were not crazies or racists but black men.[4]

At the same time, boxer Mike Tyson's hacking away parts of the ears of his opponent Evander Holyfield, another black man, in their championship match in Las Vegas in June 1997 had to rank high on the scale of brother-against-brother deplorable acts. For sports writers, boxing's money crowd, public officials, and millions of fans who watched the fight, it confirmed their public belief that one young black man (Tyson), was an animal and a savage, and their private belief that many more were just like him.

The onslaught on affirmative action, the ravishing cuts in social programs, the radical-in-reverse welfare reform law, the massive incarceration of young black males and females, and drug and gang scourge have taken a big toll on the black poor and even many in the black middle class. The joblessness rate in America for young black males remains higher than for any other group. And more young black males are being raised in impoverished, single parent homes. Despite media distortions and much of the public's belief, they are not the majority of young black males. Yet, it is risky business for policy makers to ignore the danger sign their numbers represent.[5]

◆ ◆ ◆ ◆ ◆

That was the first problem with the March. It drew largely middle- and working-class black business, professionals, academics, and students. They are the ones most likely to have stable homes, jobs, businesses, professions, trades, and the income, time, and political awareness to participate in black causes.[6]

Yet, the blacks who have turned to guns, crime, and drugs out of desolation, glamour, or the lure of quick riches are the predators who spread fear and terror in many black communities. They were the ones who most needed to be at the March. Most were not. This was not totally the fault of Farrakhan and the March organizers. They seemed to make an effort to reach the most alienated, angry, and frustrated poor young blacks. They did not succeed because many of them are way beyond the pale of militant speeches and slogans.

It would take much more than Farrakhan's attempt to shame them by branding them (as well as the blacks who attacked the March) as traitors and/or enemies. It will take specific strategies and programs to energize them and give them hope for the future. The March did not do that and it was brazenly obvious when the euphoria ended that March organizers had few clues how to do that.

Black women are reduced by far too many black filmmakers, comedians, and rappers to sluts and whores. They have been made the scapegoats for many of the crisis problems in American society. This includes many black men who blame them for their problems, too.[7]

While it was true that many black women paid public allegiance to the aims and goals of the March, privately many squirmed with unease or seethed with anger that they were not really wanted there. This agitated and intensified their ambivalence about black men. This was reflected in the poll that showed more black women were "unfavorable" than "favorable" toward Farrakhan after the March.[8]

If black women had been truly welcomed as full and active leaders and participants, they would have bulged the March's ranks. Together both genders would have unleashed and directed the energy of many black women and more black men toward cooperative work and struggle with each other. It would have insured a reliable, and stable core of thinkers and organizers. It was the opportunity of a lifetime to put the brakes on the public gender flagellation that has made much of the American public ridicule black men and women, and turn them into the laughingstock of the nation.

The failure to fully bring black women into the fold was

yet another opportunity blown. The Million Woman March in October 1997, was in large part a welcome, but far from satisfactory, attempt to correct this failure.

◆ ◆ ◆ ◆ ◆

Still, the aim of the March, which was to empower black men to grapple with their problems, was magnificent. It made many blacks see that self-help programs, voter registration, dedication to spiritual and family responsibility, and ending welfare dependency once sneered at and scorned by many blacks as the misplaced babbling of black conservatives are desirable, even necessary aims. It takes patience, dedication, and hard work; not media posturing or racially inflammatory broadsides to achieve them and regenerate a community.

For a time, after the March, some of the marchers attempted to do that. They formed a sprinkling of local Million Man March Committees, held conferences and meetings and launched voter registration drives, rallied support for small businesses, mounted campaigns against drugs and gang violence, and marched for affirmative action.

Some March activists smartly resisted the temptation during the 1996 presidential election to call on blacks not to vote or to ladle out delusions of forming a black political party. Some took a failed stab at hammering out a "black agenda" to get the attention of Republicans and Democrats. The media, black elected officials, and established black leaders ignored them. In November, blacks once again loyally cast their votes for Clinton and other Democratic candidates. But the March was loosely credited with prodding thousands of black men to vote in many cases for the first time. This bodes well for the future.[9]

Also, filmmaker Spike Lee did his bit and tried to put a positive spin on the March. His commemorative film, *Get on the Bus* in 1996, focused on a group of black men challenging themselves on the meaning of being black and male in America. Sadly, many blacks who acted out their usual love-hate with Lee, backbit him and the film and stayed away in droves from the theaters where it played. Many preferred to get their cheap thrills from sexual spectacles in films like *Booty Call* and *How To Be A Player*. This does not bode well for the future.

The efforts of Lee and the March activists were the exceptions. Many blacks treated the March like a rock concert or revival. They enjoyed the show, patted, and hugged themselves, called it a symbol of black male power, and then went home and did nothing. The initial burst of enthusiasm has long since died. Black organizations, neighborhood groups, block clubs, PTA's, churches, and social service agencies still beg for more black males to get involved with their programs and activities.

The Million Man March made many black men understand that they must work harder to better their communities. Those that are doing that work would have embodied the real spirit of the March, even if there had never been a March.

A Final Comment: Despite its towering flaws, the Million Man March inspired and spurred many blacks to make changes to improve their lives and strengthen their communities. It was and remains a solid model for local organizing. It bears rethinking how its mission for change can be transformed into a permanent mandate for change.◆

3

The Air Jordan Effect

Many blacks, young and old, are hopeless sports junkies. They passionately believe that sports is the big ticket out of the ghetto for many black youth. Why do they think this? Why do they elevate black sports superstars to Demi-Gods? Is there anything that can or should be done to break the cycle of sports delusions that many blacks promote among and about themselves?

I know that when the words sport and icon are uttered, the first name that comes to mind in the 1990s is the Air Man, Chicago Bulls basketball all-everything, Michael Jordan. But I do not think of icons or him, when I think of blacks in sport. I think of former University of Nebraska running back, Lawrence Phillips. He was arrested and sentenced to probation and counseling for assaulting his girlfriend in 1995. He was suspended from the football team. When Nebraska coach Tom Osborne reinstated him there were howls of outrage from the media and campus women's groups. Osborne did not relent. Phillips went on to have a big game in Nebraska's championship victory over Florida in the Fiesta Bowl in January 1996.

Phillips had barely stripped his uniform off when Osborne told him to "go pro." Osborne claimed he told Phillips that to save him from further difficulties if he stayed at Nebraska. The line was as good as any.[1]

Osborne certainly must know that the average shelf life of a pro football player is three to five years. With no degree, no professional training, and no real future, what will ex-jocks like Phillips do when their playing days are over? Osborne got his national championship, massive media exposure, a huge revenue boost for his football program, and a continued inside track on blue chip high school recruits.[2]

Phillips and company made all this possible. Now he was expendable. That word "expendable" may have even more meaning for him than others since his off-the-field troubles followed him into the pros in 1997. In fact, if Phillips was not careful, he would find it is only a tiptoe away from trading a football uniform for a prison uniform. While Phillips's off-the-field antics of drunk driving and probation violation are seemingly an extreme case, the plight of former black jocks is not. Thousands of them are rudely dumped after the coaches have squeezed the last inch of athletic mileage out of them. I know. It happened to me.

I starred in football in high school and college. Books were a vague after thought. Coaches fawned over me as long as I produced on the football field. When I was injured that all changed. My football usefulness had ended. After a tormenting first year in college, I was put on academic probation. The coaches and alumni were suddenly too busy to help me find a tutor, mentor, or get proper counseling. I learned the hard way that without a degree and professional training my career prospects were dim. Unfortunately, at the time, there was no one like tennis great Arthur Ashe to tell me that.

Although Ashe attained fame in the country club sport of tennis, he had no illusion that fan adoration meant racial acceptance. Immediately after he publicly disclosed in 1992 that he had AIDS, a reporter for *People* magazine asked him:

"Mr. Ashe, I guess this must be the heaviest burden you have ever had to bear?"

Ashe did not hesitate:

"You're not going to believe this, but being black is the greatest burden I've had to bear. Even now it continues to feel like an extra weight tied around me."

Ashe was troubled by the groveling adulation of super-stars by many young blacks. He felt their importance to the black community was vastly overrated. During visits to black high schools he was thunderstruck by "the obsession with sports that borders on pathology." Ashe understood that while society was ultimately to blame for transforming superstar athletes into storybook legends, many blacks have gazed rapturously at that mirage.[3]

◆ ◆ ◆ ◆ ◆

This tells much about the other worldly intoxication of sports. For many it blurs the line between reality and fantasy. Many blacks march in lock step with colleges to blur the line even more. The reason is simple: money, money, and more money. Duke, Notre Dame and UCLA are among the *creme de la creme* of NCAA Division I schools. They rake in about $15.5 million annually in sports-related dollars.

While these schools brag, with some degree of truth, about the high number of athletes that they graduate, the bottom line for the amount of money that these schools kick out for athletic scholarships is still paltry. They, in 1995, spent only $2.6 million on average for athletic scholarships. For the rest of the Division I schools, the figures are not much better and in many cases much worse. The $600 million that athletes get for their education yearly is dwarfed by the nearly $50 billion that goes for grants, scholarships, and other academic awards (and believe it or not that still includes considerable dollars for minority scholarships).[4]

The aspiring Jordans and pro footballers such as Deion Sanders spend countless hours mastering their dribbling or ball carrying skills with little thought to their future after their sports days are finished. They live for the day when they will sign stratospheric pro contracts. Their heads are stuffed with the visions of the dollars that dance through their heads and are further swelled by scanning the *Forbes* list and seeing that the richest athletes in the world are black. They hungrily look at Jordan, who took home a hefty $12.6 million in salary in 1996, and pocketed about $40 million more on the side in endorsements. (Mike was slipping. He was only the number two money maker on the *Forbes* list in 1996. In 1995, he was number one on the *Forbes* list. He was beaten out this time by the other big money Mike (Tyson) who hauled in $75 million)[5].

If their name is not Mike or Deion, a black player can still make far more than a good living—at least for the years that they play—in sport. In 1996, the NBA average pay was $2 million; the minimum is $247,500. The NFL average pay was $767,000; the minimum $131,000. In Major League Baseball, the average pay was $1.1 million; the minimum was $150,000. That is only the start for the lucky few. Baseballer Ken Griffey, Jr., basketballers Anfernee Hardaway and Shaquille O'Neal took in $5 million in 1996 in footwear endorsements alone. Jordan, of course, is still the reigning king of the endorsement hill. Nike dished out about $30 million per year to him in 1996.[6]

Most black athletes will never get these big paydays playing games. The chance of a black high school athlete making it in the pros from any sport is one in 18,000 in 1995. Only 2.3 percent or 215 of the 9,500 college football seniors will be drafted by the NFL. And the odds are 250 to 1 that a college basketball player will ever wear an NBA jersey.

37

The chances of black ex-jocks owning, running, managing, or working in a non-player capacity for pro teams are equally dreary. There were no black football, baseball, or basketball owners at the end of 1997. There were few black baseball managers or football coaches. There was one black team doctor in baseball, none in football, and only a handful of black team trainers in all the sports combined.[7]

Do not expect black press sports writers to point out this sad state of affairs. For the most part, they are not there. In 1994, there were 268 baseball beat writers listed in the Major League Baseball media guide, exactly one was black. Three years later, when Major League Baseball owners made much hoopla and fanfare on the fiftieth anniversary of Jackie Robinson's smashing the color barrier in baseball, the number of black baseball beat writers had soared to the staggering total of four.[8]

That is not where the real money is made anyway for non-players. In 1996, there was $14 billion yearly involved in product marketing, franchising, leasing, and sports agentry in the big three pro sports: baseball, basketball, and football. Professional sports owners and players have not moved mountains to help blacks get a piece of that lucrative action either. Of course, it takes capital, connections, and clout to crack this rigidly closed circle. Most blacks, or whites for that matter, do not have those connections. But many blacks do, and they are still endlessly stonewalled when it comes to getting the league owner's to believe that they can deliver.[9]

The plight of the black sports agent is even worse. In 1996, blacks made up 79 percent of the players in the NBA, 65 percent in the NFL, and 18 percent in baseball. In almost all cases they were represented by white agents. The black agents blame the black athletes for not giving them the chance to represent them and hint that they are hypocrites to boot. Said one agent, "Players wear Kente Cloth and talk about pride in their heritage, but when it comes to business affairs they don't use African-American lawyers, agents, or accountants."[10]

In most cases he is right. This is the classic case of some black athletes believing the proverbial saw that "the white man's ice is colder." Many simply do not believe that a black agent can get the owners to shell out Jordan-type dollars for them. In some cases they are right. Top-gun white agents are better connected and positioned. They have instant entree to the country clubs and boardrooms where the big greenback deals are cut, and can better deliver the goods.

Black athletes know that their time in any sport is numbered in pitifully few years, sometimes months, and they must grab as many dollars as they can, and grab them quick. But some black agents have been wildly successful in squeezing big dollars out of owners for black superstars. Their mission is to make more black athletes think that they can do that for them, too.

Dipping down in the ranks, with the arguable exception of basketball, the colleges do not do much better in promoting equal opportunity. They are so bad that the Department of Justice under pressure from Jesse Jackson's Rainbow Coalition asked the Department of Labor in 1994 to investigate the discriminatory hiring practices in the athletic programs at twelve Division I colleges. It did not. Or at least the Labor Department did not tell the public what, if anything, they found.[11]

One can tell this sorry tale of smashed hopes and dreams until the moon falls from the sky but it will not matter to many young blacks. In 1996, a group of black high school athletes were told that the odds against them making a professional team were nearly impossible. Fifty-one percent still believed that they could beat those odds. [12]

This might all be worth the sacrifice if colleges would educate them. Many still refuse. The report card on the graduation rates for black athletes at fifty Division I schools was an abomination. The majority of the schools so far during the 1990s graduated less than one-third of their black players. Four graduated none. The coaches and administrators at these schools go through verbal contortions in an effort to rationalize their failure to educate their athletes. They insist that the non-graduates transfer, drop-out of sports or turn pro.[13]

This is nonsense. Only a tiny percent of the more than 8,000 players are eligible for hardship status in the NFL. Few of them choose it. Hundreds of college players will fight for the two or three openings on each NBA team. Most of the athletes do not transfer. Those that drop-out succumb to the torrid pressure of trying to juggle practice and travel with their supposed classroom duties. Many athletes waltz through three or four years at colleges and still emerge as educational cripples, with a curriculum filled with physical education, crafts, and piles of general studies courses.

♦ ♦ ♦ ♦ ♦

Some black coaches are troubled that many of their black "student athletes" end up in dead-end jobs, no jobs, or a desperate and unlucky few land on the streets hustling or dealing drugs. From 1993 to 1995, they waged a titanic struggle against the NCAA's attempt to decrease the number of athletic scholarships, and lower academic restrictions. They were not completely successful. This was bad—and good. Many of the coaches were well-intentioned and sincerely concerned that blacks get the opportunity to attend college.[14]

Even so, there was still the suspicion that their loud protests may have had less to do with their concern about winning grades in the classroom than winning games on the court. If they were merely interested in stuffing as many black high school point guards and power forwards into their basketball team's uniforms, then their protests should have fallen on deaf ears. If the black coaches wanted players to be players and not scholars, it is understandable why.

They, like white coaches, are forced to keep their eyes transfixed on the win column. If they do not, and their losses pile up too high, their eye will be transfixed on the want ads. After all, winning is a business and a black coach, with little margin for error or incompetence, had better make it his or her only business.

Anyway, it serves little purpose to single out black coaches for the academic washout of legions of black players. Many other blacks are equally deserving of blame for sowing fields of delusions among young blacks about sports. That includes many black parents, relatives, friends, associates, teachers, and counselors. Okay, that includes just about any and every African-American who has ever turned on a TV set and marveled at Tyson soaring to the bank.

As Ashe had worried, many blacks elevate black sports heroes to Olympian heights for a very good reason. Athletes are the ones who most visibly seem to embody the much prized and the qualities of masculinity, toughness, money and power, and the independent lifestyle much denied to black men. As all imaginary heroes do, they offer momentary pleasure and vicarious escape from life's drudgeries.

Black superheroes add the special sweetener that their success symbolizes defiance of the racial codes and barriers of white society. Take a cursory glance at the pantheon of black sports figures that many blacks have propped up on the hero pedestal from ancient times to the present. They are: Jack Johnson, Joe Louis, Sugar Ray Robinson, Josh Gibson, Satchel Paige, Willie Mays, Frank Robinson, Reggie Jackson, Muhammad Ali, Julius Irving, Jim Brown, Mike Tyson, and of course, Michael Jordan. These legendary names are more than evidence of the dreamy comfort many blacks get from reveling in their triumphs and wallowing in their exploits.

All of these men, of course, have had their down moments, some very down. And that should be a reminder that sports icons are fragile. Golden State Warrior's guard Larry Sprewell can testify to that. In a rash and stupid act, Sprewell choked and threatened his coach. His multi-million dollar contract, and all pro status meant little. He was savaged by the fans, sports writers, and the media. The National Basketball Association's commissioner swiftly dumped due process for him and summarily bounced him from the league. He eventually got his day in court. But the verdict in the court of public opinion still stood. Sprewell was a "gangster" and a "thug" who got what he deserved. Society can break them at any time. Even when it does not, there are the ever present prudent warnings. In April 1997, golfer Tiger Woods stunned the golf world when he broke golf legend, Jack Nicklaus's record and became the first African-American to win the Augusta National Master's Tournament.

In interviews afterwards, Woods did and said everything right. He was properly mindful and respectful of the black golfers who in the era when golf was regarded as exclusively a rich, white man's game, were barred from golf tournaments, and forbidden to join country clubs. He was lionized by a seemingly grateful nation and dubbed by a doting Oprah Winfrey as America's favorite son. He will rake in millions in commercial endorsements.[15]

Yet the inevitable signs cropped up immediately that success can be temporal even for the most talented and deserving. His triumph may not be the magic key to unlock the door to riches for other blacks in the sport which is as close as America probably ever will come to having a sport of kings.

His father-mentor, Earl Woods noted, "This is the first black intuitive golfer raised in the United States. Before black kids grew up with basketball, football, or baseball from the time they could walk." The elder Woods recognized the pitfall of the favored sports for most young blacks and not-so-subtly tried to distance Woods, Jr. from it and them.[16]

It did not quite work. Woods had barely donned the green jacket that symbolizes the Master's Tournament crown when he got the nasty jolt that he was not the favorite son of everyone in America. Wisecracking golf ace Fuzzy Zoeller, in a TV interview, referred to Woods as a "little boy" and got off a couple of other racially-loaded slurs.

Zoeller was criticized by some in the sports world, and promptly canned by the company for which he served as a spokesperson. A properly perplexed Zoeller quickly apologized, and Woods, still basking in adulation, shrugged off the incident. Unfortunately, much of the public did not. They were outraged not at Zoeller, but at how he was treated.

Sports announcers nationally reported that pro-Zoeller sentiment was building fast. Most thought he was persecuted by the politically correct crowd for making a humorous remark that meant no harm, and blamed the media (and by extension blacks) for making a big deal out of it. So did Fuzzy. A week later, he whiffed which way the wind was blowing and turned defiant. Fuzzy cracked the same bird brain joke again to a black golfer, and for good measure added, "It still seems to me we have to stop being so sensitive about things."[17]

Not to worry. A look around the green and the club house at the Augusta National the day after Woods triumphed and one would see that there were a large number of blacks at the Augusta National. But not as golfers. They were there as caddies, waiters, and trash collectors.

Maybe in time that will change. The Woods flap was still another reminder that African-Americans must demand that high schools and colleges educate and prepare black athletes for careers outside of sports, FIRST.

This was certainly a reminder for Woods. The Stanford University drop-out seemed to understand that fame can be as fleeting as a missed putt or two. In an interview, he cautioned, "Golf is fine, but education is still the most important."[18]

As a demonstration of his sincerity, he said that he planned to finish his studies. Even he had no delusions about the Air Jordan effect.

A Final Comment: There are many African-American parents who understand that it is far more important to hold coaches, teachers, and counselors accountable for their children's performance in the classroom than their performance on the athletic court or field. They need support and encouragement. They too have no delusion about the Air Jordan effect.◆

4

Chasing Conspiracy Shadows

Far too many Americans long to believe that their are conspiracies everywhere and about everything. Many African-Americans are no different. They believe that there are secret plots, hidden plans, and quiet machinations to wipe them out. What did America do to make them think that? How much of their conspiracy fears are based on reality? How much of them are based on paranoia? Will those fears ever end?

I was amazed at two things that occurred within the space of three months of each other in late 1996 and early 1997. The first was when drug kingpin Ricky Ross was the telephone guest on a radio talk show on a black-owned station in Los Angeles. The second was when Coretta Scott King, the widow of Martin Luther King, Jr., sat in the witness box in a Memphis courtroom demanding a new trial for her husband's convicted assassin.

Ross, a convicted drug dealer, had received a mandatory federal sentence without the possibility of parole. He was one of the central characters in the alleged CIA-Contra-black drug dealer connection that government critics charged pumped massive amounts of cocaine into black neighborhoods of Los Angeles during the 1980s.

During the radio interview, Ross spewed apologies and *mea culpas* about his actions and wailed that he was a pawn of the government and that the CIA "made him do it." This was predictable coming from someone who lived a lavish lifestyle, owned millions of dollars worth of property, banked millions dealing deadly drugs in his own Los Angeles community, then got caught, convicted, and slapped with a mandatory life sentence.

While it was painful to listen to Ross's face-saving apologetics, it was even more painful to listen to black callers sidestep his guilt. Although one or two callers refused to swallow Ross's "CIA made me do it line," they reminded him that he was vile, greedy, and did not know or care who supplied his drugs. He didn't give a damn whom he hurt.

The rest of the many callers charged that the crack scourge was part of a genocidal plot by the CIA and other unnamed government forces to wipe out African-Americans. The issue of black culpability, personal responsibility, and punishment for drug dealers was buried in the rush to flaunt the conspiracy line.

This was just enough to make the alleged CIA-Cocaine connection the *cause celebre* for the black conspiracy theorists. They dropped "alleged" or "suspected" when they discussed the issue. They ignored the fact that reporter Gary Webb, who broke the story in the *San Jose Mercury News* in August 1996, did not explicitly charge that CIA officials directly conspired to, or approved, any plan to deliberately heap drugs in L.A.'s black neighborhoods.[1]

Webb made a compelling case that following a Congressional funding cut-off to the Contras in the early 1980s, key operatives within the Nicaraguan Democratic Force, one of several Contra factions organized and bankrolled by the CIA, with Reagan administration approval, for a brief time supplied cocaine to a willing Ross to raise money for equipment and weapons to keep their illegal war against the Sandinista government going. At the time Ross was apparently unaware where the money was going. Webb did not say, nor should he have implied as he unfortunately did in his series, that the CIA was directly involved in dope sales in the ghetto.

If Webb's allegations, as far as they went, had been confirmed, and there is strong inferential evidence that they were close to accurate, it meant that at least some CIA-connected operatives turned a blind eye to the dirty deals. It was not smoking-gun proof of direct CIA official involvement, let alone proof that there was a massive government conspiracy to dope-up black communities. Still, it was enough to justify outrage from all Americans. The drug plague has

49

slammed many families hard, created chaos with many lives, and allowed vote pandering public officials to turn public hysteria over drugs into public approval for harshly punitive drug laws that target minorities and the poor.

Yet many blacks shot themselves in one foot by side-stepping the culpability of men like Ross and pounding on the conspiracy theory with only the flimsiest of evidence. They shot themselves in the other foot by making the patently false claim "that *everyone* in the black community has been affected by the crack plague." This reinforced the stereotype that the drug problem is exclusively a black problem.

This is wrong-headed for another reason. It has been repeatedly found that black high school seniors were the LEAST likely group of students to use cocaine. And that cocaine use, crack or the powdered kind, was far higher among whites than blacks. Only a small percentage of the population in all communities use illicit drugs.[2]

By sprinting to judgment and not instantly distancing themselves from the conspiracy theorists, some very well-intentioned black activists and elected officials gave much of the media the excuse it eagerly wanted to attack their credibility, downplay the drug issue as a black problem, or ridicule it as yet another case of "black paranoia." This allowed the Clinton administration to ignore the charges, the Justice Department to dodge them and, CIA officials to deny them. It prevented blacks who wanted the appointment of a special counsel to fully investigate the charges from gaining broad support from elected officials and from the general public, and prevented the full prosecution of any public official or private citizen involved in drug trafficking.

The issue was left to wither on the vine within and without the black communities with no official action ever taken against any of the culprits that may have operated with the quiet government seal of approval and were actually involved in the drug trafficking.

◆ ◆ ◆ ◆ ◆

That is only one danger of overplaying the conspiracy card. During a question and answer period after a talk I gave to a small group of African-Americans in 1996, the issue of the burning of black churches came up. I pointed out that nearly one-third of the 112 arrests made by the FBI and Bureau of Alcohol, Tobacco and Firearms agents through 1996 in the burning of over 200 churches were of blacks. While in some of the cases there was strong evidence of a conspiracy by a disjointed group of racist whites to burn black churches, this could nor should not let the blacks that burned the churches off the hook.[3]

There was nothing racial about their motives. They burned their churches out of: revenge, anger, to conceal thefts, or to perpetuate insurance fraud. They were criminals and no one should try to excuse or justify their shameful and debased acts. Disappointingly, one person did. A young man in the audience immediately jumped to his feet and angrily said, "How do we know that they actually burned the churches? The only thing we have to go by is the white man's word."

The white man's word? What about the word of some of the blacks accused of arson, and that included a few black ministers. I pointed out that they actually admitted their crimes. This did not shake him. He continued to stubbornly insist that ALL the burnings were part of a racist plot to terrorize African-Americans. A few of the others in the room murmured and shook their heads in agreement with him. His blindness to reality and the agreement of some of the blacks in the room with him, was the ultimate in collective denial.

It did not surprise me. Whenever an African-American winds up in front of a court bench these days, I can predict that more than a few African-Americans will shout that they are victims of a racist conspiracy. It is a good, if not well-worn, ploy that some black politicians in defense of their own crimes have raised to a state-of-the-art enterprise.

Former Illinois Congressman Mel Reynolds shouted "racist conspiracy" when he was indicted, tried, and convicted of criminal sexual assault charges. Washington D.C. mayor Marion Barry shouted "racist conspiracy" when he was indicted, tried, and convicted on a drug charge. California Congressman Walter Tucker shouted "racist conspiracy" when he was convicted of bribery charges. Other black elected officials have loudly shouted "racist conspiracy" when they are accused of, or nailed for, sexual hijinks, bribery, corruption, or illegal campaign spending.

Yes, most of the black officials prosecuted during the late 1980s and early 1990s have been Democrats, and yes, most of the prosecutors were Reagan-appointed conservative Republicans.

It took no creative imagination to believe that some of the probes of the black lawmakers walked the thin and often misty line between the legitimate concern with bagging lawbreakers and racially-motivated political harassment. They also may have anticipated that the press would apply its customary racial double standard of saturating the public with sensationalist features and exposes of high-profile blacks accused of, or suspected of, committing crimes.

However, like the young man who adamantly disbelieved that blacks would or could burn their own churches, some blacks offered a barrage of excuses to pardon them. Some shrugged and said, "Well, they are only doing what white politicians do." Sure, but does that make it right? If it is a crime when whites do it, even if some turn a racial blind eye to their lawbreaking, it is no less a crime when blacks do it. Let's forget the moralizing for a moment. There is a practical reason why this argument should sink fast in the water.

Black politicians have a special duty to the black community. Many blacks view them not as politicians, but as leaders and advocates. They look to them to represent their interests and to challenge and confront institutional power. When they take bribes, they betray the trust of African-Americans. They should not be treated as objects of pity, folk heroes, or latter day Robin Hoods persecuted by the white establishment. They are crooks and blacks must not be afraid to say so. When they do not, it discredits them and their cause even more.

Still, some blacks say, "What do you expect, blacks are newcomers to politics and for the first time they have an opportunity to stick their fingers in the illegal political cookie jar, so they do." That excuse should sink even faster than the first one. The blacks who have been convicted of wrongdoing are not Johnny- and Jane-come- latelys to politics. Most are old Democratic party war-horses. They knew well the political ropes, and thought they could get away with illegal activities without hanging themselves. They were wrong. And other blacks should not tie themselves to the same gallows rope.[4]

To accuse much of the media or witch-hunting government officials of applying racial double-standards, and demand that government law enforcement agencies prosecute *all* lawbreakers the same, is fair and just, but that is not the same as condoning criminal behavior because those prosecuted are black and the system is perceived as racist. This is a crucial distinction that many black conspiracy theorists refuse to make.

◆ ◆ ◆ ◆ ◆

The assassination of Martin Luther King, Jr. is another matter. From the day that King was shot dead on the balcony of the Lorraine Motel in Memphis in April 1968, conspiracy theorists have sped off to the races. They claimed that James Earl Ray was a Lee Harvey Oswald-type patsy and that King's killing was orchestrated by the government. While the King family, over the years, almost certainly, and justifiably, have had private doubts about the circumstances of the murder, publicly they kept silent. That is until January 1997. Convinced by "new revelations" from Ray's attorney that the FBI and government agents were directly involved in the killing, the King family joined the ranks of the conspiracy buffs and publicly campaigned for a new trial.[5]

There is no proof that the FBI or other government agents killed King. Because of the ferocity of the FBI's secret war against King and the many questions the FBI probe left unanswered, there is just enough of a cloud of doubt that still hangs over his assassination to make many blacks believe that there was a grand government plot to slay the dreamer. Much of the FBI's dirty tactics are by now well-known. They deluged King with wiretaps, physical surveillance, poison pen letters, threats, harassment, intimidation, and leaks of his alleged sexual frolics to the media intended to smear him, his family, his associates, and by extension the civil rights movement.

To top it all off, FBI director J. Edgar Hoover whose paranoid obsession with King has been well-documented, did not explain in his agency's final report why Ray had unlimited funds to travel within and outside the country for a year with no visible means of employment. There was no deep probe of Ray's link with white supremacist groups inside the prison where he served time and on the outside. The FBI downplayed evidence that a group of Memphis businessmen financed some of Ray's ventures.[6]

Even if the answers smacked of a cover-up or a sloppy investigation, it is not the neon sign needed to prove a direct government conspiracy to murder King. The worst that could be said is that the climate of suspicion and hostility that the FBI and other government agencies created toward the civil rights movement made it possible for Ray to murder King. Ultimately, they must share at least some of the blame for that.

◆ ◆ ◆ ◆ ◆

It should not startle anyone that there are many blacks willing to claim that the despicable drug crimes in black communities of a Ricky Ross or James Earl Ray's murder of King are part of a secret master plan to annihilate blacks. Since the 1960s, the conspiracy theorists have pumped the idea that everything that happens in and to African-Americans is part of a secret plan. Their theory goes like this. Following the urban uprisings of the 1960s, the ghettos were flooded with drugs, alcohol, gangs, and guns. During the 1980s, AIDS was imported in. The "white establishment" wanted to stop blacks from developing unity, strong political organizations, and programs to counter oppression. The plot was to get blacks to self-destruct. There is no hard evidence that any of this is true.

It is, though, a mistake to malign, and make fun of the conspiracy theorists, as much of the mainstream media takes wild pleasure in doing, as kooks and crazies. The conspiracy bug is not solely a malaise of black Americans. The woods are full of whites who also believe in secret government plots and hidden global master plans to enslave loyal, red-blooded, white Christian Americans. And there is the old line that even paranoiacs have enemies.

56

With blacks, it has been publicly documented that:

• Army Intelligence, the Justice Department, and the FBI spied on black leaders and organizations between World Wars I and II.

• Federal health officials for decades knowingly withheld curative medical treatment to a group of black men in Alabama suffering from syphilis.

• The FBI conducted a massive surveillance campaign against Malcolm X, the Nation of Islam, the Black Panther Party, and other black groups in the 1960s.

• The Justice Department initiated dozens of corruption probes against black elected officials between 1983 and 1988. As already noted, there are some inferential signs that this was a punitive campaign by some Republican conservatives to traumatize black leadership.

This does not prove that there are tightly organized conspiracies or secret plots to commit genocide against blacks, nor should it excuse or absolve blacks of criminal wrong doing. By definition a conspiracy involves a small group of individuals who think alike, who have a specific objective, concoct a secret plan, and possess the power to carry it out. The Nazi slaughter of the Jews and the U.S. Government's World War II internment of Japanese-Americans are often cited as examples that can apply to African-Americans. They do not. In Germany, the Nazi Party had a small membership, a maniacal leader, a ready made blueprint for extermination, a specific target—the Jews, and most importantly, it controlled state power.[7]

A small group of American extremists did not shove the

57

Japanese-Americans into "relocation centers" during World War II, the federal government did. It played on war hysteria and racism to invoke emergency powers, gut civil liberties, and confiscate the property of Japanese-Americans. The states, the courts, and public opinion supported the action. Internment was politically unjustified and morally reprehensible. But, it was a temporary, hastily drawn-up measure, that was more overreaction to the crisis of war than a designed plot.[8]

The German and European Jews and Japanese-Americans were easily identifiable and made up a relatively tiny percent of the population of their countries. They had almost no political power. They could not turn to their government, the courts, or the media for redress. All avenues of legal protest were closed to them. That is not the case in present-day America.

The assorted white supremacist-tinged Militia, Patriot, Aryan Nation and Brotherhood groups arguably fit the conspiratorial bill. They operate in small clandestine tight knit bands, advocate a white, Christian America, have stockpiled arsenals, and conducted military drills. Some Republican party politicians have latched onto their movement to win votes or build political reputations. These groups and individuals, however, do not plot in the secret chambers of government or corporate boardrooms. They cannot move and manipulate people around like pieces on a chessboard. They do not hold state power.[9]

There is no consensus by *all* whites that African-Americans should be exterminated or locked-up in concentration camps. White opinion about blacks covers a wide gamut from sympathy to hostility to indifference.

Certainly, the current political landscape for many blacks is bleak. But, there is no defined plan to annihilate blacks. The pattern, if it can be called that, is likely to remain a haphazard mingle of economic and political gains for the black middle class, further economic deterioration for the black poor, and police and political repression for black dissidents.

Government agencies in America do occasionally play fast and loose with the law and even the rules of democracy, and their reckless actions damage people's lives. This is just enough to make many blacks panic, circle the wagons, and see hidden plots everywhere. It has been said time and again that Americans have a special affinity for a paranoid style in times of real and imagined crisis. African-Americans, like many white Americans, are no different. [10]

A Final Comment: African-Americans must recognize that many of the problems that confront African-Americans are in reality American problems. This demands that great care always be taken not to substitute paranoia for caution and vigilance, and risk turning potential friends among blacks and non-blacks into sworn enemies.◆

5

"O.J. Is Guilty"

Despite what the media believed and wanted the public to believe, many whites thought O.J. was innocent, and many blacks thought he was guilty. Why did the media distort its own polls on O.J.'s innocence or guilt among blacks? Was this symptomatic of a racial party line in America? Why do so many Americans still believe that all blacks think and act alike on racial matters? And worse, why do so many blacks think they should think and act alike?

I meet friends at the Boulevard Cafe on Sunday mornings once or twice each month for breakfast. Over the years, the Boulevard Cafe has become one of Los Angeles's most popular informal meeting places where local blacks gather to catch up on daily events, discuss issues, and exchange gossip. It is not uncommon for a celebrity or star athlete to stop in. This particular Sunday I was stunned when O.J. Simpson strolled in with some friends, and casually took seats at a corner table. It was the week after he was acquitted of the murders of his former wife, Nicole Brown Simpson and Ron Goldman.

A few patrons rushed to his table to get autographs and shake his hand. Many, however, ignored him. I also noticed that a few patrons, despite being nudged by their friends to go shake his hand and wish him well, did not budge.

I then remembered that a few months before his acquittal I watched on TV a young black man, at a vigil held for Ron Goldman and Nicole Brown Simpson on the first anniversary of their murder, gently put his arm around Fred Goldman, Ron's father, and tell him that he, and many other blacks, thought that "O.J. is guilty." It was obvious that he was not an isolated voice. I know because I frequently pleaded with some blacks to reserve their judgment on O.J.'s innocence or guilt until they had heard all the evidence and testimony. But, many African-Americans still were convinced that O.J. was guilty. They were ignored by the media.

Before the criminal trial *CNN, Time* magazine, *Newsweek* and the *Los Angeles Times* polls reported that whites believed the case against O.J. was strong. Forty-five percent of blacks disagreed. The majority of whites said that he would get a fair trial. The majority of blacks said that he would not. The case appeared to sling shot many blacks and whites to separate planets that were in no danger of colliding. *Newsweek* pronounced the O.J. case a symptom of the deepening "racial divide over Simpson's guilt or innocence." They asked blacks and whites, "Was O.J. framed?"

In July 1994, *Newsweek* was appalled that a "staggering" sixty percent of blacks agreed. What was so staggering about that? Sixty percent was hardly an iron-clad majority, let alone representing a consensus of opinion among blacks about the case. Still, the media had its story line: blacks thought he was innocent, and whites thought he was guilty. It fit neatly into the media image of a racially fractured America.[1]

In May 1995, *Newsweek* again asked blacks and whites about Simpson's guilt. Fifty-six percent of blacks thought he was not guilty. *Newsweek* again declared that blacks and whites were oceans apart in their view of Simpson's guilt. But, fifty-six percent hardly indicated anything approaching consensus on his innocence.

The polls were always less a referendum among blacks on O.J.'s guilt than the criminal justice system. Many did not believe that a black man, even a wealthy and famous celebrity like O.J., could get a fair trial. This did not mean that they believed that he was incapable of committing murder.

The media also did not look closely at its own polls. They found that a solid thirty to forty percent of blacks publicly stated, and never wavered from it during the entire O.J. legal saga, that O.J. was guilty. Privately, the numbers were even greater. Many blacks I talked with about the case as it progressed continued to tell me that they had serious doubts about O.J.'s innocence or said that it was "probable" he was guilty. Their reasons were: he had a terminal case of "jungle fever" obsession with his white ex-wife, Nicole. He was a spoiled and pampered athlete who could not take rejection. He had a history of domestic violence. The DNA tests on the blood found in O.J.'s Bronco and at his estate were conclusive proof of his guilt. Others merely said it was O.J. because there was no one else.

Many blacks were not prepared to ignore the mountain of seemingly compelling circumstantial physical evidence and testimony the prosecution presented during the criminal trial. They were convinced that O.J. strung the case out as long as he did because he was able to afford a dream team defense. They believed, and rightly so, that the average black defendant without Simpson's means would have been swiftly convicted and even more swiftly sentenced.

Even before the prosecution finished presenting its case, there was a noticeable tidal shift in black opinion on the case. More blacks openly said on black (and non-black) radio talk shows that Simpson was probably guilty.

There were two compelling reasons why many said he was guilty. The first is they believed in his guilt for some of the same reasons that many whites rabidly believed in it.

• Violent Crime. Blacks are scared stiff of it, too. Crime is an intensely personal and emotional issue for all Americans, who are angry and outraged. While many blacks, like many whites, have wrongly translated their fear of violent crime into fear of black men, the fact is that black males, at least according to official statistics, do commit a disproportionate amount of crime. The fear of black male crime no longer is taboo to discuss openly among blacks. It is a perceived reaction to danger.

• Media Manipulation. Much of the media subtly, and sometimes openly, conveyed the message that O.J. was guilty. The public expected him to be convicted, and that included many blacks.

• Domestic Violence. It is epidemic in American society and cuts across class, race, and income lines. Still, the O.J. case brought the issue to public focus. Women's groups prayed that O.J.'s conviction would send a powerful message that violence against women would no longer be tolerated. That included many black women who are just as likely to be battered or assaulted as white women. Some black women expressed their unease that the issue of domestic violence was given short shrift in the criminal trial.

• Class Resentment. O.J.'s pockets bulged enough to hire a "dream team" defense, and a small army of expert witnesses and investigators. Most blacks cannot afford to dream about that, let alone afford it. In many cases, when they are arrested they must rely on underpaid and overworked public defenders or court appointed attorneys to defend them. Their trials will not drag on for weeks or months but end quickly. The odds are that they will be convicted. O.J. confirmed their belief that justice is for sale and that the rich and famous, even

65

the black rich and famous, can always weasel out of punishment.

• Sense of Fair Play. Many blacks also get a sick feeling when they feel that someone gets away with wrong doing. While many personally admired and cheered Johnny Cochran, some still believe that he and the other Simpson defense attorneys used a smoke and mirrors strategy to confuse, distort, and obfuscate the evidence in hopes of convincing some jurors of O.J.'s innocence. The attorneys succeeded beyond their own wildest dreams, and convinced the jurors that there was reasonable doubt about his guilt. While many blacks rejoiced at the acquittal this in no way changed the fact that many of them still felt that O.J. got away with murder. The media spotlight on the suffering of the Brown family and the emotional appeals by the Goldmans that the trial was a travesty of justice touched many blacks, too.

◆ ◆ ◆ ◆ ◆

The second reason that many blacks said he was guilty had less to do with crime and punishment than it did with O.J. They did not like or respect him. He has spent much of his professional career in the "white world." He appeared to avoid publicly speaking out or embracing black causes and issues. Many blacks who publicly supported him during the trial, privately bludgeoned him for turning his back on the black community.

His well-timed photo-opish, post-acquittal appearances before black church and community groups did not convince them that he had rediscovered his roots. He had loaded up too many racial penalty points. He can make future amends only by publicly embracing and speaking out on black issues. If he does not, many blacks will continue to brand him and other black super-star athletes and entertainers who do not openly identify with the black community as racial Judases.

Is that fair to impose this racial straightjacket on O.J. and other black celebrities? Actress Barbra Streisand embraces women's causes not because she is a woman but because she believes in them. Actor Robert Redford embraces environmental causes not because he is a liberal Democrat but because he believes in them. Actor Charlton Heston embraces conservative political causes not because he is a Republican but because he believes in them. Former actress Jane Fonda at one time embraced radical causes not because she was married to a radical activist but because she believed in them.

Black athletes and entertainers Arthur Ashe, Muhammad Ali, Mike Tyson, Oprah Winfrey, Magic Johnson, Bill Cosby, Jim Brown, Reggie Jackson, Whitney Houston,, and Dave Winfield to one degree or another have embraced black causes not solely because they are black but because they believe in them. If they got involved in causes simply to pass a racial litmus test it would be a cynical and a hollow gesture.

Fame and celebrity status do not endow or bestow an obligation to social activism on anyone, nor does it entitle them to be called a leader or spokesperson. If they speak out under duress on issues they barely understand, do not really

67

believe in, and have no solutions for, then they do more harm than good. They would raise false expectations, quash hopes, and aggravate frustrations. Many African-Americans would feel manipulated and used.

If O.J., before his tumble to the depths of a disgraced and a fallen hero, had devoted his time and money to social causes strictly to appease the black critics, get added publicity mileage, or to ingratiate himself to African-Americans, I guarantee that when the pressure was off and the cameras were gone, he would have been too. Yet that was exactly what many blacks seemingly expected him to do as the price for their support.

◆ ◆ ◆ ◆ ◆

Pitiably, many legal and media commentators ignored or deliberately distorted these hidden sentiments among many blacks. They brought their own spin that blacks were hopelessly blinded by racial loyalty toward a "brother." They confidently predicted that the black jurors would never vote to convict him.

There is not a shred of conclusive evidence that blacks will knee-jerk vote to acquit black defendants out of racial allegiance. Blacks are aware that once in the jury box they are under greater public scrutiny to make sure that they do not tilt toward black defendants. They listen intently, and often put more emphasis on the evidence presented by prosecutors, and on the testimony of victims and the police than the defendants.[2]

The jurors in the Simpson case were legally and morally duty bound to honestly weigh all the evidence. If there was reasonable doubt of his guilt they had to acquit him. If there was not, they had to convict him. Obviously, they believed the former was the case.

Although the O.J. trial jurors brought down the mania of the nation on their heads for acquitting O.J. in courtroom after courtroom around the country, black jurors since the Simpson verdict have and will continue to convict black defendants, recommend stiff sentences, and in some cases vote the death penalty. That applies to celebrated black defendants as well. The sorry debacle of the other fallen from grace luminary, Illinois congressman Mel Reynolds, played out roughly during the same period as the O.J. case. There were six African-Americans on his jury and they wasted no time voting to convict him of sexual assault charges.[3]

If O.J. had not had his wealth, fame, and a top flight defense team working for him, almost certainly the jury he had would have voted to convict him, too. Even now, there are more than a few blacks who stop, turn their heads, point their finger and whisper "guilty" when he walks by. The media ignored them. But, they were there all the time.

A Final Comment: The fact that many blacks felt O.J. was guilty (just as many whites felt he was innocent) was a stark testament that things are never as simple as some badly try to make them out to be when it comes to issues of race in

America. If one had bothered to look one millimeter beyond the media obsessed, black and white, poles apart spin, one would have found that blacks like many whites had a divided mind on the case. The racial moral of the O.J. story is that trying to pigeon-hole blacks or anyone else for that matter, on an issue is like trying to stop the roaring sea with a sand castle.◆

6

The Five Dilemmas
of Black Leaders

Who speaks for African-Americans? Better yet, should anyone speak for African-Americans? Many have tried but few have succeeded. Still America's political establishment and much of the media keep trying to appoint and anoint a chosen leader for blacks. Why is this impossible to do? Is there a crisis among those blacks who call themselves or are called black leaders? Who would they lead? And what and where are they leading them to?

I always thought that white Southern-born writer Robert Penn Warren had a lot of gall to ask the question nearly a half century ago, "Who Speaks for the Negro?" The question is, and will always be, silly and presumptuous. No one asks who speaks for whites, Latinos or

Asians? No matter whether it is blacks or non-blacks, no one individual or organization can speak for an entire group. The notion of a common leadership for blacks feeds more than an ageless myth. It exposes major dilemmas confronting black leaders.[1]

This presents the first major dilemma for black leaders: Racism.

It masks the wrenching divisions of class, politics, gender, and ideology among blacks. Those divisions have repeatedly ignited fractious conflict and frantic jockeying for leadership. A century ago black scholar/activist W.E.B. DuBois challenged Booker T. Washington. During the 1920s, DuBois and labor leader A. Phillip Randolph challenged black nationalist Marcus Garvey. During the 1940s singer/radical activist Paul Robeson and the black Communists challenged the NAACP. During the 1960s Malcolm X, the Nation of Islam, and the Black Panthers challenged mainstream black leaders, Roy Wilkins, Martin Luther King, Jr., and Whitney Young.

The black militants branded them as "Uncle Toms" and "house Negroes" who sold out the black masses by pushing integration and non-violence. The militants claimed to speak for the black urban poor and workers who felt economically marginalized and alienated from the civil rights movement. They suspected that when the civil rights leaders finally broke down the racially restricted doors of corporations, government agencies, and universities, middle-class blacks, not the black poor, would be the ones who scrambled through. On this latter point they were right.

72

The murders of Martin Luther King, Jr. and Malcolm X were the turning point for the black movement. Without a leader to command the respect of the black poor and middle class and a cohesive program to unite them, the black movement plunged into a disastrous tail spin. The self-destruction from within and political sabotage from without of organizations like Student Nonviolent Coordinating Committee (SNCC) and the Panthers in the 1960s, dispirited many of their supporters and left the black movement even more organizationally fragmented and politically adrift.

The civil rights movement, too, was a victim of its own success. When it battered down the last barrier of legal segregation, the obstructionist white Southern politicians, nightriders, police dogs, and redneck sheriffs vanished from public view. They were the easy symbols of white oppression that blacks easily rallied against.

As America marched quick step into the computer and technological age, thousands more low-skill workers became obsolete. The black poor, lacking competitive technical skills and professional training, became expendable jail and street fodder and were crammed even further into the outer frontier of society. Many turned to gangs, guns, and drugs to survive.

Facing the mounting crisis, mainstream black leaders continued to backpedal. The NAACP, Urban League, and SLC exchanged the nickels and dimes it received in support from blacks for decades for corporate and foundation megabucks. They tailored their programs to accelerate opportunities for businesspersons and upwardly mobile professionals. The chase was on for SBA loans, scholarships, and

73

grants to pricey universities, corporate managerial positions, and suburban homes.

The black poor increasingly measured their plight not by the economic measuring rod of white society, but by the conspicuous gains and consumption of the black middle class. The latent class divisions burst into gaping fissures between two black Americas, one poor, desperate, and angry, the other prosperous, comfortable, and complacent. Although many among the black middle class are constantly haunted by the thought, and burn inside with rage, that as a self-designated, black privileged class their privileges could be rudely jerked away at any time.

◆ ◆ ◆ ◆ ◆

This presents the second major dilemma for black leaders: How to win political concessions from the Democratic party (or, if possible, the Republican party) and for what, and for whom, they should win them?

The sad truth is that in the last half century blacks have narrowed their political options down to essentially one: the Democratic party. That was on pitiful display at the NAACP's annual convention held during the midst of the 1996 presidential elections. The mostly black delegates stomped and hooted "four more years, four more years" as a grinning Bill Clinton stood on the speakers podium. They had no choice. Clinton had read the polls. He knew that nine out of ten blacks liked him and rated him higher than Louis Farrakhan or Jesse Jackson. But he knew much more.[2]

• In every presidential election in the past three decades blacks have given the Democratic presidential nominee more than eighty percent of their vote. They did the same for Clinton in 1996.

• The Republican party has systematically rejected blacks for three decades. They did the same in 1996.

• There is no present possibility of, nor reason for blacks to try forming an all-black party to challenge the Democrats and Republicans.

The fight for political empowerment by some black leaders did not include an active battle to support increased funding for jobs, skills training, health, education, drug and crime prevention programs, non-punitive welfare, and criminal justice reforms. This is the type of broad agenda that could appeal to both the black poor and black middle class. Instead, many black leaders cradled even more cozily into the Democratic party and pared their demands down to more party appointments and political offices. Some black leaders became even more mainstream and less responsive to the neediest, and most dispossessed in black communities. They got less rather than more political representation.

◆ ◆ ◆ ◆ ◆

This presents the third major dilemma for black leaders: The thunder on the right and the challenge from the self-styled new breed black conservative leaders.

In recent times, the biggest thunderbolt of all has been hurled by black Republican congressman J.C. Watts. After his election from a predominantly white district in 1994, the former University of Oklahoma footballer immediately threw down the gauntlet to black Democrats. He proudly and defiantly crowed that he would not join the Congressional Black Caucus.

In one of the keynote addresses at the Republican convention in 1996, Watts threw down the gauntlet again to the old line civil rights leadership. He struck a couple of the cherished conservative hot button chords: "We don't define compassion by how many people are on welfare or live in public housing—but how few."[3]

In February 1997, he threw down the gauntlet again to black Democrats and civil rights leaders when he gave the Republican rebuttal to Clinton's State of the Union address. He labeled them "race hustling, poverty pimps." It was a dirty low in mud slinging and the reaction was swift and deservedly harsh. A somewhat chagrined Watts and his Republican mentors rushed to do damage control and claimed that he was not talking about any one leader or point-of-view in particular. He was, and anyone even remotely familiar with the political battle between liberals and conservatives that bothered to think about his words knew who they were and what they represented, i.e., liberalism and blacks.[4]

There were several reasons that Watts felt comfortable enough to launch his attacks on the traditional black leadership. He knew that about one-third of blacks publicly call themselves conservative and many more blacks privately agree with some, most, or all of what men and women like Watts have to say. He also knew that the old line civil rights leadership is in crisis. They have been relentlessly battered and bruised during the 1980s and 1990s by conservative politicians and a lack of meaningful leadership. Much of the public has turned hard nosed against increased civil rights protections and more social programs. These leaders have felt the criticism and wrath of many blacks who are mortally disillusioned with two party politics and convinced that they have not, and cannot, deliver the goods.

Watts and the black conservatives believe time and the abyss-like financial pockets of Republican conservatives are on their side, that more blacks will eventually rally to their banner, and they will pick up the shattered pieces of the old black leadership. The problem they have is that while they tag traditional black leaders as the purveyors of "plantation politics" and call them sycophants of the Democrats, the majority of blacks *are* Democrats.

Though a number of blacks have reservations, if not outright doubts, about affirmative action, welfare, and other government social programs, they are not prepared to dump these programs. Watts and company are, while in the process they offer nothing better. Their politics and leadership are just as "plantation" as the black Democrats they gleefully lambast.

Civil rights leaders and black Democrats under no circumstances will run the risk of being called sell-outs and traitors by many blacks. They will continue to ignore, bait, and name-call black conservative leaders, "Uncle Toms," and

"Stepinfetchits" for the white man. Black conservative leaders under no circumstances will run the risk of being called sell-outs or traitors by their Republican henchmen. They will continue to bait and name call traditional black leaders as "bankrupt" and out of touch. In the meantime, more and more African-Americans will write both of them off as ineffectual leaders.

◆ ◆ ◆ ◆ ◆

This presents the fourth major dilemma for black leaders: The anointing of the chosen leader.

Many black personalities have knowingly played along, for personal ego strokes and material gain, with the media game of perpetuating the fraud of the "monolithic black community," and christening a "leader" to speak and act on its behalf. The media shoves the "chosen black spokesperson" into the spotlight and pretends that issues not sanctioned by the "chosen one" are not issues. It is then free to ignore any and all local leaders, actions, agendas and causes it does not like.

Much of the media, the public, and many politicians use the words and deeds of the "chosen one" as the standard to judge how African-Americans think and act. When he missteps, he becomes the hand-made whipping boy to publicly attack blacks. Cynical politicians on the right and left in the Republican and Democratic parties delight in using this tactic with the "chosen one." Each time blacks are forced to waste precious time and energy defending him and themselves from attacks, or must distance themselves from him. And each time the issues get hopelessly muddled or deliberately lost.

Many African-Americans have learned nothing from this history and must therefore bear some of the fault for this. They continue in their infinite search for the knight on the white horse to rescue them from poverty, racism, and oppression. They blindly put their faith in the "chosen one." This creates martyrs, shattered hopes, blind anger, and political paralysis. King and Malcolm X proved that. Their murders left the black movement aimlessly afloat and black leadership in chaos. Two generations later, blacks have still not recovered. When blacks reduce leadership to star and celebrity gazing they pay a dear price.

◆ ◆ ◆ ◆ ◆

This presents the fifth major dilemma for black leaders: young blacks.

Many of them are in open revolt against the older generation of black leaders. That is because no group has suffered more from the leadership malaise of the 1980s and 1990s than them. Black leaders have dismally failed to provide them with any credible role models, sustained economic and social supports, or to be big brothers, big sisters, Dutch uncles and aunts to them, to nurture and mentor them, to teach them to take pride in the heritage of struggle and accomplishments of past generations of blacks, and to understand that their struggles opened many doors for them.

79

Instead, many black leaders react to them with fear and horror at what they see as the decadence of young blacks. They degrade them, lampoon their music and lifestyles, call them derelict and irresponsible, claim they lack self-esteem, demand more police, prisons, tough laws, and the national guard to control them.

Many young blacks, in turn, are contemptuous of the hypocrisy and corruption of many black politicians and organizations. They see them wrapped in scandals, and seemingly endlessly grasping for sex, cash, and comforts. Some young blacks react by drifting into a state bordering on anomie or social withdrawal. Others become true menaces to society and prey on their own communities.

Still others take refuge in the shock-rap "gangsta" street culture and elevate fallen rap idols and thugs to sainthood. The names of the rap groups tell their tale of rebellion: Naughty by Nature, The Dogg Pound, Niggas With Attitude, Bitches With Attitudes, and Public Enemy. Rapper/actress Queen Latifah pointed to the personal and social desolation many young blacks feel, "I get depressed sometimes when I look at what the future seems to hold for us."[5]

Older black leaders are unable or unwilling to try and understand what these young men and women feel. Many young blacks are unwilling to believe that they could understand even if they tried. The only exception for some young blacks is Farrakhan. He is their hero. He appears to be the only black man willing to stand up and talk back to "the man." He captures their spirit of rebellion and defiance. His respect level jumped even higher among them in April 1997 when he got a bevy of Rappers to meet in a "Summit" following close on the heels of the murders of Tupac Shakur and Notorious B.I.G., and pledged to stop the blood-letting. His star soared even higher among them when he publicly promised to convene a rap/hip-hop summit to mark the second anniversary of the Million Man March in October 1997.[6]

He is the rare exception. For them he is probably a plausible exception because once many young blacks get beyond the music, tough talk, media swaggering, posturing, hip-hop ego gratification, fadism of Rap, and the wannabe "gangstas" that they most admire, the bitter realization strikes them that their Rap hero-leaders have no real answers or solutions for their problems either.

The economic, social, political, and generational schisms within and without black America are broad. Mainstream black leaders, "gangsta" rappers, hip-hop icons, and black conservatives, are in an intense regatta to find workable programs and strategies to deal with the crippling internal crisis of blacks, young and old, rich and poor. Whoever can find them, still will not or cannot be the answer to the odd ball question, "Who speaks for the Negro?" They will, however, be able to say that they speak for those African-Americans who agree with their philosophy and adhere to their program. That is all they could or should be able to say.

A Final Comment: Many local black leaders have found, or are coming very close to finding, practical strategies and programs that improve and enrich their communities. These leaders work quietly in the shadows, away from the glare of the media. For the moment, I will not say who I think they are, what they are doing, and what they can do more of. That will come in a concluding chapter. I will, however, say that I think they are the best answer to the question, "Who speaks for the Negro?"◆

7

Farrakhan:
The Ultimate Dilemma

Nearly every African-American has an opinion on
Nation of Islam leader Louis Farrakhan. The hate-
fascination with Farrakhan has been the longest running racial passion play in America during the 1990's.
What is behind the Farrakhan mystique? Why is he
the man black America loves to hate, or hates not to
love? Is he the genuine heir apparent to Malcolm X
and Martin Luther King, Jr.? What real threat does he
pose to mainstream black leaders?

I deliberately did not include Nation of Islam leader
Louis Farrakhan among the dilemmas that confront
mainstream black leaders. He is much more. He is their
ultimate dilemma.

He appears to give lie to the old quip that the last true leaders that blacks had lay in the graves of Malcolm X and Martin Luther King, Jr. The Nation of Islam leader seems to offer viable solutions for the black poor and to many in the black middle class. When the crowds grew big at the Nation of Islam rallies, mainstream black leaders panicked. While they had the political and economic brawn, Farrakhan had the numbers. Not only did he seem to win the hearts and minds of the black poor, his message also resonated with many middle class blacks. Partly because many face a shaky corporate future and fear that they might soon be deposited in unemployment lines. And partly because of radical chic.

The favorable opinions of many in the black middle class about him represents yet another one of the curious paradoxes that always seem to trail Farrakhan. The greater the education and greater the income of blacks, the greater the rhetorical attraction of Farrakhan to them. It is an old phenomenon that can be traced back to Garvey and has carried through Malcolm X. While many in the black middle class publicly hammered Marcus Garvey and Malcolm as demagogues and hate mongers, privately they loudly chortled when both rhetorically sledgehammered the white man. They see Farrakhan the same way, as a militant, uncompromising leader who will not do the bidding of the white establishment (or as some blacks erroneously think, the "Jewish establishment").[1]

The Million Man March made mainstream black leaders even more edgy about him. His favorable rating among all blacks immediately afterwards jumped to nearly fifty

84

percent. Some black politicians, religious leaders, and academics that bristled publicly whenever Farrakhan's name was mentioned threw in the towel, for the moment anyway, and endorsed or joined the March. They sniffed which way the breeze was blowing and knew that this was going to be a happening, a big happening, and they had to be there or lose their last drop of credibility. Even Colin Powell wavered and thought for a second about attending. He did not, but after making the obligatory denunciation of Farrakhan as a racist and anti-Semite, he still managed to say a kind word or two about the March's intent "to uplift black men and uplift African-Americans."[2]

The March was only the culmination of a leadership battle between Farrakhan and mainstream black leaders that had flared up in 1994. Then NAACP executive director Ben Chavis broke ranks with mainstream leaders and publicly announced his intention to invite Farrakhan to participate in an African-American leadership summit. All hell broke loose. Mainstream black leaders broke out in a tense cold sweat. They were now faced with their worst nightmare.

On the one hand they were under withering pressure from Jewish and white liberal and conservative political leaders to vigorously denounce Farrakhan and to boycott any meeting that he would attend. These men and women were in no mood to accept any weak-kneed, half-baked double-talk from black leaders. They reminded black politicians that they needed white political and economic support on issues vital to the black communities.

If the black leaders caved in to their pressure they would be wide open to the ancient charge that they served at the pleasure of whites who dictated to them what they could talk about and who they could talk to. Their ordeal was compounded by the realization that if they did not give in, and attended the conference with Farrakhan, it would confer the cloak of respectability on Farrakhan and undercut their own carefully crafted leadership standing. It would be tantamount to slitting their own throats. If they condemned him his popularity as the man who could not be bought or bossed almost certainly would glide even higher among millions of blacks.

What to do? Some black leaders chose to do and say nothing and hope that the storm would pass. No luck. Some finally came up with the idea of a "covenant" with him. It was purposely vague. It satisfied few. It dodged the question: What role for Farrakhan?

Whichever way it went, Farrakhan was the big winner. He was impeccably affable and gracious as ever, extended the olive branch of friendship to black leaders, and showered them with effusive praise. He told one interviewer: "I don't feel that we can go down the road to liberation without a Congressional Black Caucus or an NAACP. I feel that not only do they have something to offer me, but I have something to offer them."[3]

Farrakhan got his meeting. Some mainstream black leaders came, others damned him and stayed away. Even if the controversy had never arisen in the first place, Farrakhan still remained the tender Achilles heel for black leadership. He had powerful and troubling assets that they did not have and could not hope to have.

• <u>International Stature</u>. Farrakhan trod the path of Malcolm X and has deliberatively cultivated radical Third World leaders. His much criticized trips to Africa and the Middle East, and repeated meetings with Libyan strongman Mumamar Kadafi during the 1980s and 1990s sent the State Department into a tither, but it played well among some blacks in America. This seemed to mark him in their eyes as a world statesman that political leaders, from dictators to presidents, respected.

After he returned from his much touted World Friendship Tour in January 1996, he scored two other big international coups. The United Nations Correspondents Association invited Farrakhan to make an appearance at the United Nations. The same month the beleaguered and discredited U.N. General Secretary Boutrous-Boutrous Gali, who had been the subject of a long standing campaign by the United States to get rid of him, made what had to be a last ditch act of desperation to try to win another five-year term. He announced that he would ask Farrakhan for help. It was much too late. Boutrous-Boutrous was soon ousted.[4]

• <u>Independent Organization</u>. The Nation of Islam is the oldest exclusively black political/religious organization in America. And Farrakhan is its boss. It is, at least as far as can be determined, totally self-financed by blacks. It has not changed one word, or even a comma, in its program on paper since the earliest days of its chief architect Elijah Muhammad in the 1930s. The ideology of black nationalism has been a powerfully mystifying and enrapturing force that for two centuries has been a mainstay among many blacks. They flock to embrace it in times of acute racial hardship and when they feel especially put upon by whites. The Nation is the best known modern-day exponent of black nationalist philosophy.

The Nation has never come close to delivering on its promise of establishing the farms, factories, and banking network that would make blacks totally independent and self-sufficient in America. Its economic and social programs have at times been shrewdly shrouded in vagary making it difficult to measure results. But the followers of the Nation have started enough stores, restaurants, communications operations, anti-drug and crime programs that it appears that the organization is sincerely trying to fulfill its promise of salvation. This is just enough to keep the organization's faithful and its many admirers believing that in time it will fulfill its promise.

• The Media. It is locked in a seemingly never ending hate-fascination dance with Farrakhan. As the man everybody loves or loves to hate, he makes smashing copy. When things get slow in the pressrooms there is always a Farrakhan story to dig up. Though he protests that he is not a media hog, Farrakhan knows that he has star power appeal with much of the media and is not shy about using it to his advantage.

• Jewish Leaders. Many of them are locked into the same hate-fascination dance with him. The script goes like this: Farrakhan makes an anti-Semitic utterance—Jewish leaders reflexively attack him—Farrakhan fires back—the press frolics in the controversy and jumps on the bandwagon—blacks get mad and defend him. This has been one of the longest running passion plays in recent history, with no end in sight.

Despite these assets there are some tricky bumps in the road for Farrakhan. Many blacks still see the Nation stuck in the tight straightjacket of religious dogma and sectarian ideology, not to mention anti-Semitic and racial bigotry. There were more low grumbles from some blacks in February 1997 when some conservative Republican big shots floated the trial balloon that Farrakhan might be good for the Republican party (The Republicans finally said no). The low grumbles turned into noisy growls when he met with and addressed an annual gathering of Republican party executives and investors in Florida in March 1997. Many blacks scratched their heads and openly wondered what he expected to gain by cavorting with right-wingers?[5]

Farrakhan still needs to find allies among mainstream black leaders to ease these fears and prove that the Nation can broaden its program to reach all segments of black America. The Million Man March seemed to ratify him as the "black leader." But, there was yet another troubling cloud for him on the horizon. A Yankelovich-New Yorker *survey in 1996 found that while his popularity had rocket launched, so had his unfavorable rating. The only black that topped him on the unfavorable chart was predictably, and much deservedly, Clarence Thomas.*

The ostensible contradiction in how someone could be so popular and unpopular at the same time was easy to explain. It meant that many blacks could not make up their minds whether they liked him more than they disliked him. So, they told interviewers they held both views. Put another way, the poll revealed that as many blacks still rejected Farrakhan's philosophy as embraced it.

Mainstream black leaders are desperate to recapture the leadership high-ground and to rebuild the old civil rights coalition. They know they must attract, not alienate, whites and other non-black supporters. They interpret this to mean that they must blunt Farrakhan's influence. The dilemma for them is how?

A Final Comment: This is really a false dilemma for black leaders. Farrakhan has his philosophy, program, and agenda. It is not going to change and he is not going away. Instead of worrying about it and him, and worrying about reacting to him every time the media does, those who consider themselves, are considered by others, or are singled out by the media to be black leaders should worry about how to more effectively sell their philosophies, programs, and agendas to African-Americans. This is their most effective way to escape their ultimate dilemma: Farrakhan.◆

8

My Gay Problem,
Their Black Problem

America is a deeply homophobic society, and African-Americans, especially African-American men, are in many cases even more frantically hostile toward black, gay men. They are their bogeymen. Why does the gay lifestyle threaten so many black men? Why do so many blacks say that they could never consider a gay black man a "brother"? What blinds so many blacks to the fact that the biggest enemies of gays are also the biggest enemies of civil rights? What are the myths about gays that many blacks believe in and propagate?

I still cannot forget the scene I saw in a movie during the mid-1970s for two reasons. One, it was the first time that I had ever seen two men passionately kiss on the screen. Two, there was the reaction from the mostly black audience. They went berserk. They screamed, jeered, and hooted at the screen. It took several minutes for the crowd to quiet down and ushers to restore order. As I left the theater I listened to the young men talk. Their contempt and disgust for these two men spilled out into the street and into the parking lot. They called them "faggots," "punks," and "sissies." It seemed as if they were feverishly trying to scrape the slime off themselves that the scene of these two men kissing had left on them.

A year or so later, I was at a local political meeting. Afterwards, while talking with a friend, a young black man came up to us. My friend winked at me and whispered "he's a queer," and quickly walked away. I stood there alone with him. After a moment of awkward silence, we started talking. I mentioned that I was a jogger. His eyes immediately lit up. He said he was, too. He quickly suggested that maybe we could go jogging together. Even though I really did not know anything about the man and neither, I suspect, did my friend, I still froze in naked panic.

I thought about the young men who jeered the gay men on the screen at the theater. At the time, I thought that their antics were downright silly and in poor taste. I now realized that I was no different. I had the same horror of, and prejudice against gays as they had. But why? Did they threaten me? Did they stir queasy and violent passions in so many of us? Did I feel an even more intense dislike for a black man who was gay? Did they threaten and challenge my fragile masculinity at the basest and most ambiguous level? They did. And this forced me to take a deep soul search into my own homophobic fears. Even though I hated what I saw and had no rational explanation for these fears, I understood why they were buried tomb-like in me.

◆ ◆ ◆ ◆ ◆

From cradle to grave, much of America has drilled into black men the thought that they are less than men. This made many black men believe and accept the gender propaganda that the only real men in American society are white men. In a vain attempt to recapture their denied masculinity, many black men, mirrored America's traditional fear and hatred of homosexuality. They swallowed whole the phony and perverse John Wayne definition of manhood, that real men talked and acted tough, shed no tears, and never showed their emotions.

These were the prized strengths of manhood. When men broke the prescribed male code of conduct and showed their feelings, they were sneered at as weaklings, and their manhood questioned. Many black men who bought this malarkey did not heap the same scorn on women who were lesbians. White and black gay women did not pose the same threat as gay men. They were women and that meant that they were fair game to be demeaned and marginalized by many men.

Many blacks, in an attempt to distance themselves from gays and avoid confronting their own biases, dismissed homosexuality as "their thing." Translated: homosexuality

93

was a kinky contrivance of white males and females that reflected the decadence of white America. They made no distinction between white gays and other whites. To them whites were whites were whites.

Many blacks listened to countless numbers of black ministers shout and condemn to fire and brimstone any man who dared think about, yearn for, or God forbid, actually engage in the "godless" and "unnatural act" of having a sexual relationship with another man. If they had any doubts about it, they fell back on the good book. They could, as generations of bible-toting white preachers did, flip to the oft-cited line in *Leviticus* that sternly calls men laying down with men, "the abomination."

◆ ◆ ◆ ◆ ◆

While many Americans made gays their gender bogeymen, many blacks made black gay men their bogeymen and waged open warfare against them. Black gay men became the pariahs among pariahs, and wherever possible every attempt was made to railroad them out of black life.

Some of these efforts have been especially pathetic. Civil rights leader Bayard Rustin, a known gay, and the major mover and shaker behind the 1963 March on Washington, was sternly warned by some March leaders not to publicly "embarrass" or compromise the March by his personal conduct. A popular black nationalist magazine of that day took frequent and dizzy delight in calling Rustin "the little fairy." No black leader publicly challenged its homophobia.[1]

In *Soul on Ice,* published in 1969, then black radical Eldridge Cleaver viciously mugged James Baldwin for his homosexuality and declared homosexuality the ultimate "racial death wish." No black leader publicly challenged Cleaver on this point, and his outrageous fad theories on sexuality were praised by an entire generation of radical wannabes as if they were the sacrosanct word from on high.

A decade later black gay filmmaker, Marlon Riggs, hoped that the hostile public attitudes of many blacks toward gays had lessened enough to at least permit a civil discussion among them about masculinity and homophobia. In a purposely ambiguous and veiled concession to the anti-gay mood, Riggs stole a bit of the rhetoric of black militants and proclaimed that "Black men loving black men is the revolutionary act of our times." It did not work. Riggs found that anti-gay bigotry was just as entrenched as ever among many blacks.[2]

Rappers such as Ice Cube still rapped "Real niggers ain't gay" on his "Death Certificate" album. Leading Afrocentrists swore that "homosexuality is a deviation from Afrocentricity." And bushels of black ministers, with generous support from their white Christian fundamentalist brethren, still branded homosexuality "a sin before God." Some blacks escalated their low intensity warfare against gays to an all-out, take no prisoners battleground.

Nation of Islam leader Louis Farrakhan made it almost

part of his divine mission to attack homosexuality. Even though the Million Man March publicly welcomed gays and treated the ones who participated civilly, no one really believed that this represented a sea change in attitude among blacks toward gays. If some did, Farrakhan quickly wiped out that notion in a TV interview with conservative newsmen Evans and Novack in March, 1997. He made it clear that he still regarded homosexuality as an "unnatural act" and would discourage the practice whenever and wherever he could.

The traditional civil rights leaders continued to denounce homophobia, and urge support of gay rights. They reminded blacks that homophobia and racism were two sides of the same coin and that many of the same white conservatives, from Pat Buchanan to Jerry Falwell, who ruthlessly savaged gays were the same ones who ruthlessly savaged civil rights.

These leaders were right. But, their argument still cut little weight with many blacks. The one and only comprehensive survey conducted in 1995 that measured black attitudes toward gays found that blacks, like whites, had not slackened up one bit in their hostility toward gays. More damning and ominous for blacks, they still continued to heap special scorn on black gay men. The one potential bright spot in this even had a taint. The survey found that there was less anti-gay sentiment among the more educated, less religious, and more affluent blacks but ONLY if the gay male was white. They still slung black gay men far, far out into the netherworld of contempt.[3]

That anti-gay feeling runs so deep among many African-Americans that there is a virtual black-out of any discussion or activities of black gay men. Black gays and lesbians have held a number of National Black Gay Conferences since 1987. Yet, there has been only the scantest mention of them in the black press. The national gay and lesbian publication, *BLK* might as well gather dust in the Smithsonian Museum for all that most blacks know about it.

Some blacks justify the out-of-sight, out-of-mind exclusion of gay men from black life by arguing that the gay life style is a major threat to the black family. This hinges on the shaky assumption that there are thousands of gay men lying in wait to subvert traditional family values. Beyond the fact that no one really knows how many black or non-black men consider themselves exclusively gay, much of what passes for traditional family values has long been turned into shambles. The happy face Ozzie and Harriet family of the drowsy 1950s that conservatives pant away for has been totally exposed by writers as a fraud even in that day. Many men drank, gambled, had adulterous affairs, beat their wives, and kids, and took a complete hands-off-attitude toward child rearing and nurturing. Many of them were absentee fathers. The only difference is that they were physically in the home.

Even if Ozzie and Harriet was not a complete fabrication, America of the 1990s bears no resemblance to the 1950s. The majority of women must work outside the home. They are better educated, are pursuing careers in business, the professions, and the trades. They have drastically changed the shape of gender and family relations in America. There are all sorts of family combinations in the 1990s that were barely

97

imaginable a generation ago. There are single working women, single working men, grandparents, single sex male and female couples, step parents, foster parents, designated guardians, foster homes, and even children that are raising children.

If the American family still fully resembled the storybook Ozzie and Harriet family, the list of the mightiest destabilizers of the black family which many can recite by heart would still remain the same: poverty, unemployment, lack of education, chronic disease, violence, drugs, alcoholism, imprisonment, and early death. Gays are not on this list.

Black gay men continue to feel like men without a people. They carry the triple burden of being black, male, and gay. They are rejected by many blacks and sense that they are only barely tolerated by white gays. Many black gay men feel trapped, tormented, and confused by this quandary. They still spend sleepless nights and endless days figuring out ways to repress, hide or deny their sexuality from family members, friends, and society.

Black gay men worry that the hatred of other black men towards them will not change as long as they feel that their manhood is subverted, accept America's artificial standard of what a "real" man is, and anti-gay attitudes remain firmly rooted in much of the American public.[4]

This will only change when more black leaders understand that when you scratch a homophobe, underneath you will invariably find a racist. When more black men realize that black gay bashing will win no brownie points with conservatives, and will certainly not make them any more sympathetic to black causes, the better things will become. Former Nation of Islam national spokesman Khalid Muhammad found that out. In a widely publicized speech in 1993, he made one of the most devastating and disgusting public assaults ever on gays. Yet he was still one of the most vilified black men in America at the time.

The leaders of the Million Man March upheld the spirit of the March by including gays. This was a positive step in that it tacitly recognized that as black men, gays face many of the same problems as all black men. It in no way meant that the majority of black men were willing to completely accept black gay men as brothers and equals. They *are* equals and I hope that more black men are wise enough to see that they should be the last ones on the planet to jettison other blacks who may be in a position to make valuable contributions to the struggle for political and economic empowerment. It took time for me to learn all of this. But, I did, because I no longer wanted my gay problem to be their black problem.

A Final Comment: In time, more black men will come out of the closet and more black men will meet them, get to know them better as people, too, or in some cases discover that they have known them all along as a family member, friend, or acquaintance. This will force even more black men to reexamine their own defective definitions of manhood and confront their own homophobia. This will go far toward ridding them of their fear of black gays as *their* bogeymen.◆

9

The Crisis in
Black and Black

From time immemorial race has been so obsessive in black-white relations, that class has been badly ignored in black-black relations. Black class divisions have led to sometimes hidden, sometimes explosive tensions within and without black communities. What is the black vs. black class conflict? How did the black class crisis come about? How has it confused and harmed relations among blacks? Is there a solution?

I was terribly uneasy as I watched the more than 1,500 persons pack the First AME Church in Los Angeles on the night of April 29, 1992. Many in the mostly black crowd were nattily attired in tailored business suits, ties, *Yves*

Saint Laurent shirts, *Ferragamo* shoes, fashion designed skirts, elegant African gowns, *Louis Vuitton* pouches and purses. The scent of *Pierre Cardin* cologne and *Estee Lauder* perfume wafted in the air.

They were at the church to protest the acquittal by a Simi Valley jury with no blacks of four white Los Angeles Police Department officers accused of beating Rodney King. The rally had been called by the city's top black politicians, business, civil rights, and religious leaders. The crowd sat politely listening to indignant but restrained protest speeches. In between they sang and prayed.

Outside, hundreds of blacks milled about. They were not dressed in tailored business suits and fashion designer dresses. They were whipped into a paroxysm of rage at the Simi Valley verdict. Some tried to get into the church. They were turned away. They were in no mood to sing, pray or listen to genteel speeches by politicians and preachers. They felt little kinship with the well-heeled businesspersons and professionals inside. The chasm of class, status, and income between them was as wide as the Grand Canyon. They felt isolated and excluded by them. They felt their leaders had neglected and betrayed their needs and problems.

Some struck back. They burned businesses, overturned cars, and assaulted motorists. In that moment of blind fury, their enemy was not only the "white power structure" but the black middle class, too. Many blacks cowered in the church, not from fear of white police bullets, but of black street anger. The first chance they got, many blacks fled the church under protective escort, and the neighborhood in terror.

The concealed class fissures among blacks, long blurred by racism, ignored by blacks and hidden from white society, had detonated to the surface. Speaking strictly of the conflict between blacks and whites, America was no longer two nations, black versus white. America was now three nations, black versus white, and black versus black.

◆ ◆ ◆ ◆ ◆

Sociologist E. Franklin Frazier sounded the first alarm in the 1950s. In *Black Bourgeoisie*, he noted that between the World Wars hundreds of thousands of blacks escaped the poverty, peonage, and Jim Crow violence of the South and migrated to the North. In the less legally restricted racial climate of the North, many blacks found greater opportunities in business, the professions, and trades.

Frazier warned that they were becoming a prosperous "black bourgeoisie" that controlled the wealth and power within the black community and turned their backs on their own people. Worse, many members of the "black bourgeoisie" began to ape the values, standards, and ideals of the white middle class, and to distance themselves from the black poor. Frazier contemptuously called them "colored Babbits" and accused them of turning their backs on their own people, "the black bourgeoisie has lost much of its feeling of racial solidarity with the Negro masses."[1]

103

He was ahead of himself. Segregation was still the law of the land. The black bourgeoisie could not buy its way out of the ghetto. Landlords and real estate agents still refused to rent or sell homes to prosperous blacks in the suburbs.

The big change came in the mid-1960s. Federal entitlement programs, civil rights legislation, equal opportunity statutes and affirmative action programs initiated during Lyndon Johnson's administration broke the last barriers of legal segregation. The path to universities and corporations for some blacks was now wide open.

While the federal government was the big player, there were three other factors that permanently altered the character of the black ghetto: the expansion of managerial positions for college educated blacks, increased union involvement, and the continued migration of blacks from the farms of the rural South to the factories of the urban North.

The impact was phenomenal. Between 1975 and 1990, the number of black professionals, technicians, administrators, and managers nearly tripled. The number of black college graduates doubled. Black business directly profited from the surge. The administration of President Jimmy Carter strengthened federal programs that provided grants, loans, and technical training for minority businesses. By the time Carter left the White House in 1980, the federal government nearly tripled the amount of business it did with black firms—$1 billion to $2.7 billion.[2]

This triggered yet another change. Black firms muscled aside the traditional mom and pop grocery, service, retail stores, barber and beauty shops, then moved into petroleum and energy, manufacturing, automotive sales, and investments and equity trading. During the next decade and a half the number of black-owned firms doubled the growth of all small businesses in America.[3]

The Reagan-Bush administration's demolition of many job, education and social programs of the 1980s slowed but did not halt the gains of the black middle class. Black household income jumped eighty-four percent. By 1993, more than fifteen percent of black households earned more than $50,000 annually. The top one fifth of black families earned nearly half of all black income. Black wealth, like white wealth, was now concentrated in fewer hands.[4]

The members of the "new" black bourgeoisie did what their parents only dreamed of: they got out of "the hood." By the end of the 1980s, an estimated one in ten blacks were affluent enough to move to the suburbs. The expansion of tract homes, condos, and apartments made their move easier.

By the mid-1990s, the stampede from the inner city was in full swing. The term "black flight" began to creep into the media vocabulary. The new black suburbanites crossed their fingers and prayed that no one slashed their tires, tossed a brick through their front windows, or called their children niggers in their integrated classrooms.

The economic strength of the new black bourgeoisie translated into huge political numbers. Suddenly there were blacks in the Senate, more in Congress, in Bush and Clinton's cabinets, for a time in a governor's mansion, and in dozens of state legislatures and local and municipal offices nationally.

Many in the "new" black bourgeoisie figured that if they had finally attained the American Dream, the era of protest was over.

They got it partly right. The era of major mass protest may have been over but some of the conditions that sparked them were not. The wearying quest for the American Dream which contained the jumble of reality and delusion still sent many blacks into nightmarish tremors about their real and imagined treatment. They were still subjected to poor (or no) service in restaurants; bypassed by taxicabs; spread-eagled on the ground and searched by police; followed in stores by security guards; denied loans for their businesses and housing; losing ground in building their net worth assets in relation to those of the white middle class; and resegregated in formerly all-white to now all-black suburbs.

The much touted smash through that blacks had supposedly made in corporate America is still the stuff of much fiction. In 1994, there were fewer than a half dozen black CEOs at the *Fortune* 1000 corporations; white males made up 97 percent of the senior managers. Yet many blacks had moved up the ladder in corporate America, participated in company social functions, were included in discussions of vital business, and were welcomed in country clubs. Few corporate officials stoked the flames of racial hostility by repeating the tired fib that they "cannot find a qualified black." Many corporations had active minority recruiting programs.[5]

The Texaco fiasco in 1996, where some Texaco officials were caught on tape racially slandering their black employees and conniving ways not to promote them, proved that many blacks are still regarded by many of their corporate peers as social lepers. Some blacks had attained enough status in the hallowed corporate hallways that it could not be truthfully said that all of corporate America was still cloaked in a white sheet.[6]

◆ ◆ ◆ ◆ ◆

Back in "the hood" it was a different story. During the 1960s, the Vietnam war drained billions from the domestic budget, the Great Society unraveled, and the few piecemeal and badly mismanaged "poverty" programs were systematically dismantled. The ghetto uprisings sparked white backlash. The murders of Malcolm X and Martin Luther King, Jr. left the civil rights movement in tattered disarray.

Without a leader to rally the masses or a comprehensive urban program to address the surging economic crisis of the ghetto poor, civil rights organizations and black politicians did a volte face. They defined the Black Agenda in increasingly narrow terms: affirmative action, economic parity, professional advancement and busing replaced battling poverty, reducing unemployment, securing quality education, promoting self-help, and gaining greater political empowerment as the goals of ALL African-Americans.

The need for, and furious pursuit of, money and status by

the black elite not only fueled class tensions among blacks, but in some cases had deadly consequences for the black working class. A textbook example was the campaign to save black lives by getting them to stop smoking. The death rates of mostly poor and working class blacks from lung cancer, emphysema, prostrate cancer, and heart disease is double that of whites.[7]

Yet, while the tobacco industry deliberately targeted blacks in its advertisements, many black leaders, organizations, magazines, newspapers and radio stations, art and music groups for years eagerly lapped up the tobacco industry's dollars. Between 1989-1993, cigarette manufacturers such as Phillip Morris bankrolled these black organizations: National Urban League, $4.4 million; United Negro College Fund, $500,000; National Caucus of Black State Legislators, $60,000; and the Congressional Black Caucus, $155,000. The SCLC and the NAACP also tapped the tobacco till, too.

The major black magazines such as *Ebony, Essence,* and *Jet,* and black newspapers and radio stations for years crammed their pages and filled the airwaves with cigarette and liquor ads. Although they now attract more diverse major corporate advertisers, cigarette advertising still remains sure fire money in the bank for them.

The ads show chic, well-dressed prosperous looking black couples and families at work and play. This unabashed play on the image of success and upward mobility stirs fantasies of wealth and power, and rams home the message to blacks that the American Dream is only a cigarette puff away. In 1991,

Secretary of Health and Human Services, Louis Sullivan invited black publishers to discuss the adverse affects of tobacco advertising in the black communities. Not one magazine publisher and only a handful of newspaper editors showed up. Meanwhile, the black poor continued to die in pathetically high numbers from tobacco-related diseases.[8]

The insular, self-serving goals of many black leaders left the black poor not only more isolated but more at risk. The OPEC oil price rises, foreign competition, inflationary pressures and industrial shrinkage in the 1970s and 1980s ushered in the era of economic belt-tightening. The technological transformation of American industry increased the demand for an educated and professionally trained workforce. Black firms, despite their impressive growth, could not help the black poor. They were still largely economic paupers within American corporate capitalism. The 100 service and industrial companies in 1996 employed only 51,000 blacks. This is far less than one percent of the general black work force in America.[9]

The black poor, lacking education, competitive skills and training, were further hurtled to the outer fringes of society. Many others simply plunged deeper into the morass of poverty and welfare dependency.

This is the ultimate class dilemma that faces African-Americans. The black middle class could not as Frazier claimed "assert themselves or exercise power as white men do." Yet they want to. Many feel suffocated by the straightjacket of race in America. Yet they are unable to yank the straps loose. The black poor can not attain wealth or status to break their cycle of poverty and climb into the middle class. Yet they want to. Many do not want to accept or identify with the values of the black middle class. Yet they are forced to because these are the dominant values of American society that they are bombarded with night and day as the only values worth emulating. It is a match of ill-suited paramours.[10]

The black poor and the new black bourgeoisie are inseparably bound by race, and agonizingly divided by class. The black schism cannot be cavalierly dismissed or ignored with simple pleas about "black unity." The problem goes much deeper and so must possible strategies for change. It was so much simpler when the crisis was in black and white.

A Final Comment: The crisis in black and black is not a doom and gloom scenario. While class divisions have been hidden and denied by generations of academics and political leaders, they are a fact of life among Americans. It is no surprise then that African-Americans would be divided along class lines, too. This does not mean that those divisions are eternally resistant to change and that blacks of any income or status cannot find common issues they agree on and common interests to fight for.

It takes wise leaders and committed organizations to define those issues and forge a common agenda. It has been done before. The Poor Peoples Campaign led by Martin Luther King, Jr., the black pride movement, the voter rights movement of the 1960s, the independent black political campaign movement of the 1970s, the full employment campaign of the 1980s, the stop the violence movement, and the movement to stop the burning of black churches in the 1990s are just a few examples of the issues that cut across class lines and that blacks, young and old, rich and poor, have taken action on together.

It is true it was so much simpler when the crisis was in black and white. But nowhere is it written that mutual action by African-Americans cannot be taken to resolve problems, even when the crisis is in black and black.◆

10

Afrocentrism: Whose History to Believe?

For decades blacks have denounced white academics for "whitening" world history, and denying black contributions to it. But what happens when some blacks "blacken" world history and deny that whites or other ethnic groups made any substantial contribution to it? Do they substitute a feel good history for honest historical studies? Do these individuals over glorify the African past, and ignore the proud history of black struggle and achievement in America? What harm do they do to the battle for black and multicultural studies?

I, like many black high school students in the early 1960s, learned about Africa watching *Tarzan*, *King Solomon's Mines*, and *Jungle Jim*. I learned about Egypt watching the *Land of the Pharaohs, Cleopatra,* and the *Ten Commandments.* I learned about Greek mythology watching *Hercules* and *Jason and the Argonauts.* I learned about the Moors watching *Othello.* I learned about the slave resistance to the Roman Empire watching *Spartacus.* I learned about American slavery watching *Gone With the Wind.*

White actors and actresses, Johnny Weismuller, Jack Hawkins, Elizabeth Taylor, Steve Reeves, Kirk Douglas, Laurence Olivier, Clark Gable, and Vivian Leigh were my heroes and heroines, my view of the world was filtered almost entirely through the prism of celluloid Hollywood. During my first two years in college, I became well-acquainted with Italian opera, French art, English literature and theater, German philosophy, Greek antiquity, Russian classical composers, and Spanish dance.

I believed eminent historian Arnold Toynbee when he wrote in *A Study of History,* "The black races alone have not contributed positively to any civilization—as yet." Toynbee's "as yet," seemed like an afterthought that vanished fast when he tallied up the world's civilizations. He assured that Caucasians contributed to nearly all of civilization. Toynbee conceded that the "yellow" and "red" races made a few contributions. He left blacks out in the cold.[1]

Senegalese scholar Cheik Diop, disgusted with Eurocentric tunnel vision in scholarship, stood the Toynbee view of history on its head in *Civilization or Barbarism: An Authentic Anthropology.* He assured that African peoples produced all the world's civilizations. He left whites out in the cold.[2]

114

The Afrocentrists have squared off against the Western classi-
cists in the 1980s and 1990s. But, whose history to believe? Their
fight over historical truth is more than an academic contest of racial
one-upmanship. What is at stake is control of educational resources,
curriculum development, faculty slots, and the political thinking of
young activists and scholars.

Politicizing the social sciences to score racial points is
hardly new. The Afrocentrists stand on solid ground when
they charge that European and American academics still
resist the inclusion of African contributions. In 1992, *Time*
magazine did little to dispel their suspicions. In its feature
article on Afrocentrism, one writer pretended to be the even-
handed critic and gently chided Toynbee for the "bland
dismissal" of African contributions. He delivered a mild hand
slap to academics for their "racism when dealing with Africa." He then unleashed a torrent of abuse against his main
quarry: Afrocentrism. He called it a "world of absurd claims,"
and a "plague" on scholarship.[3]

◆ ◆ ◆ ◆ ◆

In the earliest charge against Afrocentrism, conservatives
tagged them the new academic totalitarians. Even this was
not enough for historian Arthur Schlessinger. In a long tirade
that bordered on personal vendetta against Afrocentrism, he
told *American Heritage* that "racism is not an invention of the
Occident." Hummm? The next wave of attackers pulled all
stops not only to denounce Afrocentrism but to demolish it.

115

Mary Lefkowiticz headed the assault. She loaded fact after fact after fact in her book, *Not Out of Africa* in 1996, to essentially prove one thing, "The ancient Egypt described by Afrocentrists is a fiction." When *Time, Newsweek, US. News & World Report*, the *New York Times*, and the *Los Angeles Times* rapturously embraced the book, that seemed to close up the shop on Afrocentrism.[4]

The jewel in the crown for many Afrocentrists and their white and black scholarly critics is Egypt. They are waging their biggest battles with the Afrocentrists for it. For decades, European and American scholars claimed that Egypt was not part of Africa but belonged to the "fertile crescent." This was an area that supposedly encompassed the Near and Middle East. *The Cambridge History of Africa* explained that the region was "peopled by Caucasians." And there was "no evidence of an African substratum in ancient Egypt."[5]

In a 1992 article, "Afro-Centrism: Hype or History," *Library Journal* gave the impression that scholarly racism was part of a dead past, "white scholars are freeing themselves from the racism and anti-Semitism that helped shape many long held views about history." This is more delusion than reality. The *1990 Funk & Wagnalls New Encyclopedia* acknowledged that Egypt was a multi-racial society. It meticulously listed and explained the contributions of Asian, Roman, Greek, Mediterranean, and Jewish history. Africans, however, were not mentioned.[6]

Africans fared little better in the 1992 *Encyclopedia Americana*. The Asian, Roman, Greek, Mediterranean, and Jewish influence in Egypt was explored in detail. There was a bare hint that one Dynasty may have been ruled by the Nubians from the South. The *Encyclopedia* called it a short, "obscure period" with no record of their achievements.

Under pressure from black scholars and activists to "clean-up" the texts and halt the bias against African people, publishers made improvements. However, many of the racial distortions, errors, omissions, and stereotypes are still present. In 1993, I examined six textbooks that were then part of the standard curriculum for Fourth through Seventh graders in California schools.

In *A Message of Ancient Days*, Africans were described as "naked dark-skinned people" who eat "bloody bones." *The Story of America*, claimed that for blacks after slavery "their African heritage all but disappeared." In *One Nation Many People*, the black communities are described as dismal havens ruled by "pushers, whores, and gamblers." Harlem was dismissed as "a pit of dilapidation and fury."

A small band of black and white scholars that included W.E.B. DuBois, Leo Hansberry, Carter G. Woodson, Franz Boas, Melville Herskovitts and Basil Davidson refuted the European whitewash. They accused Eighteenth and Nineteenth European and American scholars of deliberately creating the myth of black inferiority to justify slavery and racial oppression. They cited historical research, traveler's accounts, and anthropological studies as proof that Ancient Egypt was a multi-racial society. There were black, brown, and white scientists, engineers, scholars, administrators, and Pharaohs during each of the thirty-two Dynasties.

117

They demonstrated that West and Central Africa was not a stagnant backwater area. African peoples made major contributions and innovations in metallurgy, weaving, agriculture, and merchandising that Europeans later copied.[7]

For many Afrocentrists this is not enough. They claim that ancient Egypt was exclusively black and the world's major contributions were made by Africans. They produce their own experts and studies to show that Europeans were greedy interlopers who stole the cultural and social legacy of Africa while plundering, murdering, and enslaving its people. They draw on fresh research and interpretations to show the importance of African contributions to the West. Much of this is welcome relief.

◆ ◆ ◆ ◆ ◆

Yet in their zeal to counter the heavy handed "Eurocentric" imbalance of history, some have crossed the paper thin line between historic fact and fantasy. They have constructed groundless theories in which Europeans are "Ice People," suffer "genetic defects," or are obsessed with "color phobias." They have replaced the shallow European "great man" theory of history with a feel good interpretation of history. Reputable black scholars instantly saw the danger. They warned that Afrocentrism is not about racially reversed biological determinism but showing that Africans are subjects of history and human experience rather than objects.[8]

There are more problems. In the battle to force scholars to recognize the black contribution to Egyptian and Western civilization, many Afrocentrists minimize the contributions made by other non-whites. They also reduce West Africa to secondary importance in world development.

Even more unpardonable are the sensational, and often undocumented boasts by some Afrocentrists of mythical black achievements which permit the sworn enemies of multi-cultural studies to seize even more of the intellectual highground. They self-righteously drape themselves in the cloak of scholarly reason. They claim to defend the sacred walls of academia from the invasion by anti-intellectual black chauvinists. They garner sympathy from many college administrators and faculty members, politicians and business leaders, and much of the press.

Those who oppose stretching academic curricula to reflect the achievements and contribution to American and world history of people of color would attack multi-culturalism even if the fringe Afrocentrists did not exist. This group of Afrocentrists just make their job easier.

The final and worst snare of all is that many Afrocentrists ignore the critical role African-Americans played in shaping America's institutions. This amounts to a back door acceptance of the myth that African-American history began and ended with slavery. This massive omission scandalously slapped me in the face in January 1997, when Clinton much belatedly awarded seven African-American veterans the Medal of Honor for their bravery during World War II.

I knew that thousands of black soldiers answered the call to arms during World War II, as they have in all of America's wars. I knew that black soldiers had to wage an even more intense battle against segregation and abuse in the military.

119

Until the Medal awards ceremony I did not know that so many blacks had distinguished themselves with such magnificent heroism on the battlefield.

During the media coverage of Clinton's inauguration two weeks after the ceremony, a radio commentator casually mentioned that black slaves performed most of the labor in the initial construction of the White House. I did not know that either. I have written and researched numerous articles and several books on the black experience. If I did not know about events like these, does anyone think that millions of other blacks and non-blacks know about them either?

These accomplishments are only the tip of the rich black historical iceberg in America. Black inventors, explorers, scientists, architects, and trade unionists helped construct the foundation of American industry. Black abolitionists, religious, and civil rights leaders helped shape law, politics, and ethics in America. Black artists, writers, and musicians gave America its most distinctive cultural art forms.

This should be a point of pride and self-esteem for young African-Americans. They can identify with these accomplishments much easier than the remote and much disputed Egyptian past.

When some Afrocentrists embellish scholarship with fairy tales, they play into their enemy's hands. European and American racial propagandists got away with this for more than a century and look at the mess they made of history.

A Final Comment: Thoughtful black and non-black scholars have found several ways to try to end the racist white-out of black contributions to American and world history and the exaggerations and distortions of extremist Afrocentrists. They push for publishers to revise all classroom texts that compartmentalize black achievements into a single chapter (for example "slavery" or "civil rights") and to include them in all text chapters.

They demand that school administrators and teachers make sure that black achievements are woven throughout all classroom curricula, from science and technology to the humanities. They encourage public officials to commemorate black achievements in ceremonies throughout the entire year. They implore corporations to regularly feature black achievements in their advertising and promotional materials.

These scholars know whose history to believe.◆

11

The Concrete Killing Fields

The sad fact is that most young black males and females who die violent deaths die not at the hands of white police or white vigilantes but at the hands of other young blacks. Some young blacks have turned America's cities into killing zones. Is it enough to blame their killing on racism and poverty? Are Rap lyrics the major culprit? Is it TV violence? Is it all of the above and much more? Is there something in the black lifestyles that create a climate for violent acts?

I was puzzled why so many media sound trucks were parked in front of the gleaming building on Wilshire Blvd. in Los Angeles as I drove past on the evening of

March 10, 1997. I later learned why. Notorious B.I.G. (aka Biggie Smalls), the popular "gangsta" rapper, was slain hours before. Biggie had just come out of a party at the Petersen Automotive Museum. When the shots rang out there was bedlam and hundreds of party-goers ducked and scattered. There was no confusion about who Biggie's shooter was, "All I could see was that he was black," said Biggies, rap buddy, Lil Caesar, who witnessed the shooting.[1]

Biggie's murder followed closely on the heels of the murder of rival rapper Tupac Shakur a few months before in Las Vegas. The two men shared much in common. They were rappers. They were wealthy and popular. They were young black males. Their murderers were in most cases other blacks.[2]

They are not alone. A staggering 44,428 black males were murdered between 1980 and 1985—nearly equal the total number of Americans killed during the entire Vietnam conflict. The number of black females murdered between 1980 and 1985 exceeds the number of American casualties (9,500) in Vietnam in 1967, one of the peak years of fighting. Nearly all of the victims knew their killers, and nearly all were murdered by other blacks. This proved again that despite what much of the media says and much of the public believes, blacks are not a menace to society but a menace to themselves.[3]

The soaring murder rate is only one brutal sign of the magnitude of the violence. In 1995, blacks accounted for 63 percent of those arrested for robbery, 41 percent for aggravated assault, and 36 percent for simple assault. With the spread of the drug trade in African-American communities, the murder and violence figures have careened even more sharply upward. Presently, an African-American male is twelve times more likely to be murdered than a white.[4]

The grim death cycle is daily played out in city streets. We have seen five-year-olds "accidentally" killed in gang crossfire. We have seen parents dressing their children in bullet proof vests. We have seen countless photos of grieving families at the funerals of the young black murder victims.

While the victims and perpetrators are mostly black, white Americans are traumatized that the violence could soon spell trouble in their neighborhoods. So politicians and law enforcement officials scramble for answers.

Their answers in effect have been no answers. More prisons and more police have not solved the problem. Neither have tougher laws, dragnets, barricades, and street sweeps. Blacks are not slaughtering each other at an alarming rate because they are "by nature" violent or crime prone. They are not killing each other simply because they are "poor and oppressed." The problem is much bigger. We must look at the complex mix of social, economic, and historical ingredients that have shaped the black experience.

◆ ◆ ◆ ◆ ◆

No matter how extreme the violence suffered during slavery and the half century of segregation and peonage that followed in the South, blacks were forbidden to retaliate against whites. If they did, the penalty was lynching, lengthy

125

prison terms, or the death penalty. Meanwhile crimes committed by blacks against other blacks were ignored or lightly punished. The implicit message was that black life was cheap and white life sacred.

Time and again studies have tiresomely confirmed that the punishment blacks receive when the victim is white is far more severe than if their victim were black. This devaluation of black life by racism has had horrible consequences. It encourages disrespect for the law and has forced many blacks to internalize anger and displace aggression onto other blacks.[5]

The folklore, language, traditions, and music of blacks often reveals this covert aggressive response to white violence. Claude Brown, in his novel *Manchild in the Promised Land,* vividly described the havoc from shootings and brawls that blacks wreak on each other on Friday and Saturday nights in Harlem.[6]

Black men have become especially adept at acting out their frustrations at white society's denial of their "manhood" by carving out an exaggerated "tough guy" role. They swagger, boast, curse, fight, and commit violent self-destructive acts. When black women refuse to be sexually submissive or are perceived as trying to "control" them, they become frequent targets of the violence. Black females were four times more likely than white females and nearly 1-1/2 times more likely than white males to be murdered.[7]

When the violent implosion drives many black males and females to indulge their murderous impulses on other black males or females, they are often taking out their pent-up

126

frustrations, that have no other outlet, on those whom they perceive are as helpless and hapless as themselves. The twisted psychological forces that turn black aggression inward is not a personality flaw, racial aberration, or a product of the insupportable, but perennially popular with some sociologists and much of the media, culture of violence, or subculture of poverty theories, but more likely a warped response to racism and deprivation, blocked opportunities, powerlessness and alienation.[8]

The social and psychic empty place that many young black males experience, and its sometimes deadly and explosive consequences for other blacks, is hardly unique to the African-American experience, or even American society. Among the group that has suffered perhaps even more mightily from cultural rape and physical genocide than African-Americans are Native-Americans. The violent implosion among them is just as deadly. The aggravated assault rate of Native-American-on-Native-American on the reservations is six times the United States' rural rate. The murder rate is three times greater than that of the rural United States.[9]

The same violence-turned-inward phenomenon was also commonplace among non-whites under two centuries of European colonial rule. Psychiatrist and militant activist, Frantz Fanon first spotted the deadly cycle of repression-frustration-violence turned inward in Algeria under French colonial domination. Fanon was appalled by the high number of stabbings, beatings, and murders committed by young Algerians against other Algerians.

127

The victims and victimizers were almost always the poorest of poor young men. As Fanon noted, the Algerian dispossessed worker or peasant could not strike back at those he blamed for his plight—the French businessman, the tax collector, judge or policemen—without risk of severe reprisals. So, what did he do? He took it out on his neighbor, friend, or even family member whom he came to see in his bitter and blurred view, as his relentless enemy. Fanon noted that the Algerian-on-Algerian crime and violence level tumbled during the anti-colonial war against the French during the 1950s and early 1960s.[10]

Something similar happened in America among blacks. For a brief moment during the 1960s, the black-on-black destruction abated. The civil rights and Black Power movements channeled black anger and energies into the externally directed battle against racism and poverty. This gave many blacks pride in themselves and hope for the future. The urban civil explosions of the 1960s intensified the feeling among many blacks that they could take control of their communities and their lives.

The collapse of the civil rights and black militant movements, economic shrinkage, and government repression left the black poor without leaders or viable organizations to fight back against the raging conservative assaults on civil rights and economic gains. Despair, fragmentation, and hopelessness grew. Black youth were the biggest casualties. Gangs became an attractive street alternative. They gave many black youth security, self-worth, and their sense of belonging. Colored scarves, shirts, pants, and jogging suits became symbols of status and identification that many youths were willing to die and kill others for.

The spread of the drug trade during the 1980s made black youth gangs even bigger and more dangerous. Drug trafficking not only provided illicit profits but also made gun play even more widespread.

Gang members used their arsenals to fend off attacks, protect their profits from hostile predators, and to settle scores with rivals. Much of the escalation in the murder rates during the mid-1990s could be traced directly to busted drug deals, competition over markets, and disputes over turf. Often, innocent victims were caught in their shoot-outs, thus fueling black fears and fortifying the public nightmare that the black communities were depraved war zones.

Many blacks suspect that some police and public officials wink and nod at the violence as long as it is confined to African-American communities. They cite the ease with which black gangs get guns and drugs and swear that is part of a plot or conspiracy to destabilize African-American communities.

There is no proof that this is true. Yet it is hard to slide around study after study that show murders or physical attacks committed by blacks against whites are still punished with swift arrest, sure convictions, and longer sentences than crimes against other blacks. As long as that is the case, it will be tough to shake the belief that black life is devalued by many whites and blacks.[11]

There is one more culprit that aids and abets black violence—the media. On average, a white youth by age 12 has seen more than 40,000 murders or attempted murders and 250,000 violent acts on TV. Black youths of the same age will witness even more TV gore because they spend nearly twice as many hours in front of the tube. What does this tell them about the world? Are they to be blamed if they cynically disregard human life and accept violence as the natural order of the world?[12]

Like an executioner's deadly sword, the threat of death hangs menacingly over the heads of many African-Americans no matter whether they are Tupac Shakur, Notorious B.I.G., the kid down the street, or the one who lives in their own household. Until that threat is removed, they will continue to be shameful victims of America's concrete killing fields.

A Final Comment: Following the Los Angeles civil disturbances in 1992, Crip and Blood gang members in the South Central area of Los Angeles decided that a time to kill had ended. They declared a truce. They created businesses and jobs, warded off those who badly wanted their peace pact to fail, forced the worst cynics to grudgingly admit that the truce worked, and brought a measure of peace to their communities. They showed that weapons can be turned into ploughshares on the concrete killing fields of America.◆

12

Hollywood's Booty Call

Blacks practically bankroll Hollywood with their dollars. They buy an estimated one out of four movie tickets to all American films. What are they getting for their movie spending splurge? Do they help Hollywood reinforce the Sambo, Mammy, Amos n' Andy, "Gangsta," sexually degenerate image of themselves? Should blacks turn off to those black filmmakers who specialize in creating spectacles of degradation of blacks on the screen? Can blacks do anything to insure that black filmmakers, actors, and scriptwriters turn out positive films and TV productions that entertain AND uplift and inspire?

I talked with a friend immediately after he came out of a screening of the film, *Rosewood*, in March 1997. He shook with rage not about the film, which he considered a powerful story of the tragedy of the destruction of the mostly black Florida town by white mobs in 1923 and the quiet struggle of blacks for justice. He shook with rage in part because there were relatively few people in the theater to see it. But in bigger part, he shook because of what he heard in the adjoining theater. He sat in the back of the theater and when the theater door opened he could barely hear what was being said on the screen because of the wild shrieks and laughter from the audience next door.

The crowd there was mostly black and they were in delirium over *Booty Call*, a goof ball film about the sexual frolics of young blacks. He was not the only one disgusted by the histrionics of blacks over a mindless film like this. Bill Cosby was also livid that blacks had sunk to such a sorry and disgusting low in self-debasement. He was even more perturbed at the hare-brained, self-serving excuses that some blacks came up with to try and defend these kinds of films. He quoted one, "Would you rather me be waiting in the alley for you or making *Booty Call?*" Cosby stripped away the baloney and simply answered, "Have you looked in the papers in the want ads?"[1]

Underneath Cosby's grim humor-retort, and my friend's anger, there is the pathetic reality that Hollywood has a maddening love affair with the ancient racial stereotypes of crime/dope/guns/freaky sex/cartoon caricatures/human wrecks that it reserves almost exclusively for blacks. It knows that 1990s blaxploitation films that pump out the stereotypes, are cheaply made, and gross from $15 to $60 million. Hollywood also knows that blacks mob the theaters to see these films. They buy an estimated one out of four movie tickets to all movies made in the United States.[2]

The black filmmakers who make these kinds of films and the blacks who rely on negative stereotypes and images, cackle at their own degradation. They trot out a decrepit arsenal of myths and lies to justify their complicity in their own defilement.

• Many black filmmakers and black audiences say these films reflect the reality of the "hood."

They do not. Nine out of ten adult black males are not in prison, on probation or parole. Nearly six out of ten young blacks reside in two parent households. Teen pregnancy rates have tumbled among black girls and leaped among non-black girls. Three out of four black women have never received welfare payments. Eight out of ten adult blacks are employed.[3]

• They like to see themselves on the screen.

For six decades blacks have played cops, robbers, dope pushers, pimps, whores, presidents, mammies, corporate heads, maids, aliens, astronauts, devils, washerwomen, zombies, oodles of singers and dancers, and every role in between. By now black audiences should be mature enough to discriminate in their movie tastes and demand films that portray them with more dignity than depravity.

Other ethnics are not stuck in Hollywood's time warp. Jews want to see themselves in movies other than a *Hester Street*. Italian-Americans want to see themselves in movies other than a *Godfather*, Chinese-Americans want to see themselves in movies other than a *Shanghai Triad*. Latinos want to see themselves in movies other than an *American Me*.

• They employ black actors and actresses.

So did *Emperor Jones, Gone with the Wind, Green Pastures, Cabin in the Sky, Song of the South, Tarzan, Jungle Jim, King Solomon's Mines* and the pack of 1970's blaxploitation films. Hollywood never had a problem creating plentiful roles for toms, coons, mulattos, mammies and clowns. Despite the heavy profits in black "gangsta"-decadence films, Hollywood is not barreling ahead to bring out more black films. In 1995, it produced ten. And Hollywood showed what it really thinks of blacks in movieland when it nominated a paltry twenty-five blacks for Oscars between 1963 to 1997.[4]

Pioneer filmmakers Oscar Michauex and Haile Gerima proved that there is a better way to create cinema opportunities for blacks. In the 1930s, Michauex made independent films with a poverty budget that employed hundreds of black actors, actresses and technicians. In recent times, Gerima did not wait for or beg Hollywood to bankroll the anti-slavery epic, *Sankofa* in 1993. He proved that a commercially successful independent black film can create jobs and opportunities for dozens of blacks in the 1990s.

Actor, singer, and activist, Paul Robeson had yet another answer for those black actors and actresses who are fed up with the Amos n' Andy, gangland roles. Robeson was embarrassed by the Stepinfetchit type part he was forced to play in movies in the days (1930s and 1940s) when blacks had no other choice, because Hollywood gave them no other choice but to play buckdance roles or not work at all. So a decade later he actually picketed in front of a theater in which one of the movies he played in was showing and urged blacks not to go see it. But that was another time, another place, and Paul Robeson.[5]

• They put dollars in black pockets.

They put dollars in the pockets of wealthy investors, executives, corporations, distributors, theatre chain owners, and elite screenwriters. Winston Groom, the author of *Forest Gump*, found this out. *Gump*, the film, released in 1995 grossed $650 million. Paramount used "creative accounting" to show a net paper loss on the film. It paid Groom a measly $350,000 and paid star Tom Hanks and the director $31 million. It took negative publicity and the threat of a lawsuit to get Paramount to shell out a few more bucks to Groom.[6]

Author Terry McMillan reportedly sold the rights to her book, *Waiting to Exhale*, for the film released in 1996, for less than $1 million. The film grossed $60 million. Alice Walker thought she beat Hollywood's "creative accounting" methods when she signed for three percent of the gross revenues for Steven Speilberg's screen adaptation of *Color Purple* in

1985. The movie was a huge hit. Speilberg and Warner Bros. made a mint, and Walker by her own account got only "a fraction" of what she thought the movie earned. By contrast, New Line Cinema paid screenwriter Shane Black $4 million for *The Long Kiss Goodnight* released in 1996 and $1.75 million for *The Last Boyscout* (a flop) in 1994.[7]

◆ ◆ ◆ ◆ ◆

Meanwhile, far too many black leaders and organizations have maintained a statue like silence on these cinematic image assassinations. This is irritating, especially since they pay endless lip service to the notion of promoting black achievement and demolishing racial stereotypes. They know that many of the young filmmakers writing about the "hood" could not find a housing project or the inside of a welfare office if their lives depended on it. They know that many young blacks who flock to these movies neither live in the ghetto or have had a "ghetto experience"

They know that many young blacks are in ecstasy watching these characters swagger, posture, act tough, be defiant and sexually outlandish because they imagine that they actually are rebelling against something. They know that blacks pay a huge price for peddling stereotypes by themselves about themselves in the form of the escalating attacks by politicians on social programs, the increased racial hostility of many whites, and the massive numbers of blacks being shuttled off to prison and graveyards. Some black leaders do speak out and they should be applauded, but far too many do not, or even worse, applaud some of these cinema and TV obscenities. They should be encouraged to break their vow of silence.

A small group of NAACP rebels tried to do just that and they promptly found out that trying to wean blacks off the stereotypes about themselves is not as easy as it might seem. They denounced the NAACP Image Awards in 1997 for nominating some TV sit-coms that are among the worst of the worst manglers of the black image for image awards. The sparks flew and some NAACP officials dexterously pirouetted around the issue, but finally the deplorable portrayals shoveled out by some in Hollywood proved much too much for them.

They finally reprimanded Warner Bros. for showing its "contempt" for African-Americans by its clownish portrayal of them on its WB network. Now who will consistently reprimand those African-Americans who see nothing wrong and everything right in laughing at, and acting out, their own degradation?[8]

A Final Comment: Many blacks say that they are sick and tired of seeing themselves portrayed as clowns, crooks, and charity cases on the screen. But as long as they pay Hollywood to shape and define their image, and as long as many refuse to lift a finger and cough up a dime to support those independent filmmakers who portray them with dignity and not degradation, Hollywood will be more than happy to continue to give them a booty call.◆

13

The Return of
the Mau-Mauer

Soul singer James Brown once derided in a song those who talk loud and say nothing. He could easily have been talking about those blacks who have made their blacker than thou militancy a fetish, and take giddy delight in haranguing other blacks who do not put their color on conspicuous display. Just who are they? Should they be taken seriously? Are they doing anything to improve the quality of life for African-Americans? Do they do more harm than good to the black cause?

I have watched the ranks grow during the 1990s of some bizarre characters in the black communities. I call them Mau-Mauers. I do not mean the men and women who fought against British colonial rule in Kenya in the 1950s. I mean those blacks who perpetually preach revolution and scream "get Whitey." As soul singer James Brown put it, they talk loud and say nothing. Worse they do nothing. The term "Mau-Mauer" was first used during the 1960s to describe the pseudo-militants.

They never joined an organization, participated in a protest march, attended a rally, signed a petition, wrote a protest letter, or made a phone call. They never contributed any time or money to help a movement or cause. The black organizations were not radical enough. Their programs were bankrupt. They called all black leaders "lackeys" and "sell outs." They would have been millionaires if there had been a fire sale on the excuses they gave for their do nothingism.

In those days black leaders and activists took action in the streets, at high schools and colleges, and in the factories. They were always in the faces of the politicians and presidents. They had a philosophy or a program for nearly everyone. They preached civil rights, black power, black conservatism, communism, and armed struggle. Black organizations had concrete, practical programs that changed the social face of America. That was then. Most of the activist leaders, organizations and programs didn't survive the 1960s. Some activists were killed, compromised, self-destructed, or fell victim to their own success.

The Mau-Mauers did survive. Today their ranks have swollen. I hear them on local TV and radio talk shows. They bellyache about

140

the "white man," "white devil," white oppressor," or "white estab-
lishment." They concoct bizarre tales of secret plots, hidden agen-
das, and Jewish conspiracies. They swear that "the white man" is
preparing the final assault against blacks. He is systematically
doping them up, locking them up, contaminating them with AIDS,
or preparing to toss them into concentration camps.

I hear them on college campuses. They spin concocted
stories of ancient black kingdoms and dynasties that once
"ruled the world." They stuff their heads with fake-scholarly
books that propound esoteric, genetic, or psychological theories to explain the predatory nature of the white "beast/
devil."

They hail the avalanche of convoluted and garbled writings that few can understand, and even fewer bother to read
as the greatest works since Jehovah etched the Ten Commandments in stone. They pay handsome fees to "controversial" speakers to conduct campus feel good sessions that bait
whites or Jews. These cathartic outbursts remind me of big
tent summer revival meetings, where everyone feels good for
the moment but, two minutes after they walk out, they can not
name one practical thing they learned that will improve their
lives.

◆ ◆ ◆ ◆ ◆

I see the Mau-Mauers on TV scurrying from *CNN* to *Fox*
Newstalk peddling wolf tickets about the evil ways of white
(but more likely) black folks. If they have written a "hot" seller

141

that masquerades as an authoritative work on global white supremacy or bashes black males or females, they have an open passport to tabloid TV talk land. Blacks will stampede the book stores to add it to their shelves, where it will collect cob webs and mercifully be quickly forgotten along with the other "hot" sellers of yesteryear.

I hear them in their homes rage endlessly against blacks for spending their money with whites. This supposedly proves that blacks hopelessly grovel in self-hate.

I heard them on the streets when I was a commentator for the CBS-TV affiliate in Los Angeles during the O.J. Simpson criminal trial in 1995. They praised me for what they believed was "speaking up for the brother" and complained that the media is a brutal weapon against blacks. I thought about what the rap/poetry group, The Last Poets, said about the blacks who packed the halls to hear Malcolm X. They loved to hear Malcolm rap, but they did not love Malcolm.

The Last Poets were right. Following his assassination, except for a faithful few, Malcolm was quickly banished by blacks to the empty hole of oblivion for nearly two decades before the rappers, Spike Lee, and Hollywood in 1992 briefly turned him into a mass commodity.

Mindful of Malcolm's fate, I decided to test my black "supporters." I gave them a file card with the name, address, telephone, and fax numbers of the TV station's news director. I asked them to write, call, or fax and tell him that they wanted more black analysts, commentators, and news reporters on the station to present honest, accurate, non-stereotypical news, and features about blacks. Some did. Most did not. It is simply much easier and more fun to complain (almost exclusively and safely to each other) about the "racist white media."

That is the problem. The Mau-Mauers confuse and frustrate many blacks who want positive change and are desperately seeking direction, leadership, organization, and programs for positive change. This requires time, patience, and hard work; not media posturing, grandstanding, and rhetorical masturbation. Then again, perhaps this is the ultimate fear of the Mau-Mauer.

A Final Comment: During the movement days of the 1960s there were always far, far more black leaders and activists who did not perch on their haunches on the sidelines and complain. They gave their time, energy, and money to the battle for social change. This is still the case today. They were then and now the unsung heroes and heroines of the black struggle. They were and are the antidote to the Mau-Mauers.◆

14

Bad As I Wanna Be

> Many blacks have turned life in black neighbor-
> hoods into a tattered fashion statement. To hear them
> tell it they all grew up in impoverished crime-in-
> fested, welfare ridden, drug-reeking ghettos. They
> flaunt this image as a badge of pride to the media and
> the world. In most cases they are deliberately paint-
> ing a false picture of life for most blacks. Why do
> some blacks revel in the crime/violence/derelict im-
> age of blacks? How much fame and fortune do they
> gain from hustling the "gangsta" image? Why do so
> many Americans believe that all blacks live like this?
> What damage does image assassination by blacks do
> to all blacks?

I was one of two guests on a popular radio talk show
in Los Angeles in 1995. The subject of the program
was the depiction of young blacks in movies. The other

guest was the screenwriter for a wildly successful "gangsta" style film. I was ready to pounce on the young screenwriter for being yet another black image assassin foisting the fraudulent crime/violence/drug/derelict image of young blacks off on America to grab quick cash and fame.

I was prepared to hear him defend what he wrote with the conscience-salving line I have heard *ad nauseam* from the "gangsta" image apologists that, "I'm just telling the world about my life in the 'hood'." Mercifully he did not fish out that tall tale.

He could not, because like most young blacks this was not his life. He grew up in a stable two parent household. He was a college graduate and lived in an integrated middle-class neighborhood. He had written other scripts about teen love and family life based on his real personal experiences, but his screen agent flatly told him he was wasting his and Hollywood's time. No deal. He got the message that many in Hollywood didn't believe black families existed and blacks could fall in love like anyone else. The young screenwriter for the moment gulped down his dream and gave the movie studios the guns, gangs, drugs, and decadence they expected about black life, and they loved it.

Two weeks later, in two separate talk shows, a prominent black actor and a popular recording artist said that they were raised in a crumbling project or tenement. They did not know their fathers. Their mothers were on welfare. They fought daily battles against drug addicts, rapists, thieves, and murderers. They ran with or away from gangs. They were lucky to be alive. Their stories, along with the screen fabrication of the young screenwriter, sounded suspiciously alike. I wondered if I was missing something? Did all or most blacks grow up poor, destitute, and dysfunctional?

I thought about my childhood years in the 1960s. My parents were not rich. The neighborhood I lived in was a typical black, working class neighborhood. No one thought of it as a rotting ghetto or broken down slum. As I remember, most of my friend's parents were in the home. They worked on the railroads, in the factories, at the post office, or as domestics. They made sure their children did not go hungry and had a roof over their heads. Many of them wore hand-me-down clothes but they were not ragged and they were always clean. Most of the children managed to finish school.

We were not perennially miserable. We played games, fought and got into mischief just like other kids. Our neighborhood was not crowded with junkies, thieves, rapists, murderers, and drug dealers. There were alcoholics, drug addicts, and violent criminals but they were a small minority. Most of us had enough sense to steer clear of them and avoid that life.

A female friend remembered much the same about her childhood. She was not molested, raped, or sexually abused by a drunken or doped up father, male relative, or family friend. She knew some women who were, but they were hardly the majority.

In the 1950s and 1960s, sociologists, top-heavy with private and government grants, began branding black neighborhoods as cesspools of rot. They carved a growth industry out of studying "black deviancy" and "the pathology of the ghetto." In the 1990s a legion of pop scholars put a new twist to ghetto pathology. They did not just dissect it, they indicted blacks for creating it.

I have been accused of being incurably rhapsodic about a by-gone past and putting a happy face on ghetto life. "Gangsta" rappers, black novelists, essayists, poets, playwrights, and filmmakers insist that life in today's "hood" is a rugged survival test. The reality, they claim, is that people daily dodge bullets, go to funerals of friends and relatives killed by gangs, step over people lying in drug or alcoholic stupors, hide from rapists and molesters, and despair over absentee or abusive fathers. The true reality is that most blacks do not do any of this.

Nine out of ten adult black males are not in prison, on parole, or on probation. More than eight out of ten young blacks graduate from high school. Nearly six out of ten young blacks reside in two parent households. Teen pregnancy rates have soared among white girls but sharply dropped among black girls. In California, the black teen pregnancy rate is less than half that of white unmarried teens. Three out of four black women have never received welfare payments.[1]

Despite corporate downsizing, the conservative barrage against affirmative action, and spending for job skills training and education programs, more than seven out of ten blacks are employed. In the media's favorite "gang and poverty ridden" projects such as Cabrini-Green in Chicago and Jordan Downs in the Watts area of Los Angeles, there are many non-welfare dependent, two-parent households. The children do not sell drugs, join gangs, get pregnant, or drop-out of school.

While rapper Notorious B.I.G., who was gunned down in March 1997, worked way overtime to shove his tough guy image down the throats of a gullible public, his mother knew better, "He wouldn't hurt a fly. I want his children to see him the way he really was, a father not a rapper. He really loved his family." As much puzzled as hurt by her son's death, she was probably right about him and his real life. But B.I.G. was not murdered because of the way he really was. He was murdered because of the way others thought he was.[2]

This does not jibe with the view of the "hood" by many non-blacks, and far too many blacks. They forget, ignore, or deliberately distort the fact that more blacks do the right thing than the wrong thing. They believe and repeat mantra-like to others that blacks are poor, violent, abused, and sexually depraved. They read, hold as gospel, and regurgitate the press's tabloid obsession with crime-drug-gang-dereliction-sex-violence and depravity stories.

This obsession became heart breakingly clear when I heard that four young black men won Rhodes Scholarships in 1994. I scanned back issues of the leading black newspapers and magazines for 1994 for any mention of their feat. Other than a short item in the news brief section of the May 1994 edition of *Black Enterprise*, and a flash mention in *Jet* magazine, I found no word on the four men in any other black publication. When I casually told friends and acquaintances that four black men had won Rhodes Scholarships that year, and that hundreds of thousands of young black high schoolers compete each year in the NAACP Academic, Cultural, Technological and Scientific Olympics (ACT-SO) competition they reacted with a puzzled mixture of ignorance, disbelief, or sobering silence. Some tried to cover up their blind spot by ranting about the racial sins and crimes of the "white media."[3]

Even when some well-meaning blacks set out to set the record straight on black achievement, they often wind up purveying the same stereotypes that they are trying to dispel. In March 1997, a *Newsweek* feature article, "The Black Gen X Nobody Knows," was typical. The article started out nobly. It focused on the solid achievements of young black scholars at several high schools and colleges, but then it went downhill.

It slipped into the standard litany of mean streets, "gangsta" culture, and "at risk" myths and stereotypes about young black males, and liberally sprinkled these media formula negatives with constant reminders that this is the preordained fate of most blacks. The reader was left again with the impression that blacks who achieve and do not wind up as victims of the mean streets, are, at best, the exceptions, and at worst, freaks of nature.[4]

The media certainly has much to atone for the part it plays in reinforcing racial stereotypes and kindling public fear of blacks, especially young black males. Beating up on the "white media" misses the damaging point that much of the black press often does the same. The black press mimics much of the mainstream media and titillates black readers with crime and violence stories. It turns the much-too-familiar cast of superstar athletes and entertainers into holy idols. Then, it recycles the seemingly imperishable celebrity hero-worship stories onto black readers.

◆ ◆ ◆ ◆ ◆

Many black personalities have discovered a gold mine in pandering to the profane. Rap mogul Dr. Dre had the decency not to even try and hide his cash hunt or paper it over with the pseudo political apologetic, "I'm just educating the public about the 'hood'," when he bluntly said "I'm no gangsta; I'm here to make money." Basketball's clown-prince, Chicago Bulls star, Dennis Rodman is equally candid and unabashedly brags about romping in the gutter to reap America's riches.[5]

The same cannot be said for far too many other black personalities who carefully reassemble their past into a collection of sordid tall tales. These individuals calculate that this is a sure ticket onto sleaze talk shows, brings hefty advances from publishers, boosts record sales, and secures movie deals. A number of corporate sponsors and TV producers cement the unholy alliance with the bad as I wannabe be crowd by making them a staple of freaky daytime talk shows.

151

Trash talk TV producers count on a horde of willing young black men and women to mug and shout into the cameras on cue like trained seals and create colossal spectacles of degradation and gargantuan displays of dysfunctionality. The panelists and audience get their fifteen seconds of fame. (I would not dignify their antics with minutes since all are quickly forgotten) and America gets an Amos n' Andy, Coon, and Minstrel show.

"Gangsta" rappers, have justifiably, and in some cases, deservedly, borne the brunt of America's dump on them for creating a fabulous growth industry out of black stereotypes. The ones who have sold their people's soul for thirty pounds of silver and a little extra change deserve what they get. If they do prostitute themselves, it is because they know that rebellious young whites, Latinos, and Asians, who are almost totally mindless of the complexities of the black experience, will deliriously fork up the cash for their skewed music-video-cartoonish version of black life. And the more skewed the better.

If the shock rappers try to soft peddle their song lyrics/ thuggish image and stray even a micro inch from the "gangsta" ghetto script, the cash registers in Suburbia will go deader than a door nail and they can kiss the platinum record sales good-bye. They know that enough young blacks, who even though they do not self-describe themselves as "gangstas," are still wannabe enough to identify with their music, clothes, rhetoric, and, yes, their rap.[6]

♦ ♦ ♦ ♦ ♦

Some in the black media, some black rappers, and other random media narcissists are not the only culprits. Some black leaders encourage the bad as I wannabe crowd by playing the numbers game to magnify black misery. They endlessly tell the media how many blacks are unemployed, in prison, join gangs, peddle dope, suffer from AIDS, drop out of school, and get pregnant. They depict black life as a vast sink hole of violence and despair and portray black communities in permanent crisis and chaos.

Some of these characters snatch an occasional spot on *Nightline* or *Oprah* and shake a few dollars from the fast disappearing number of liberals for their pet programs. The doomsday scenario not only wore thin in the 1990s, it became self-defeating. Many whites believe that the problems of the ghetto are self-made and insoluble. Many politicians agree. They refuse to spend another nickel on job, welfare, health or education programs. At the same time, they have made affirmative action a dead letter, and demand more police and prisons. In poll after poll, young, and not so young, whites, persist in believing that blacks are: (a) lazier, (b) more crime prone, and (c) less American (i.e., not worthy of the same rights and privileges as them).

The fall-out from this has been almost as great among many blacks. They have become cynical. They refuse to support black organizations or causes, circle the wagons in their businesses, professions, or neighborhoods, and frantically distance themselves from the black poor.

153

Trading in stereotypes about themselves may make the world believe that blacks are bad as they wannabe be and may be hip, cool, and profitable for some blacks. It may even nab them an occasional guest spot on *Oprah* or far worse, the sorry lot of freakier-the-better TV talk shows. But, most blacks pay a steep price for it. And there is nothing good about that.

A Final Comment: What is good is that many African-Americans emphasize in words and deeds what African-Americans are doing right and not wrong. They do not assassinate their own image. They are the ones who should be listened to.◆

15

The Fallacy of Talkin' Black

Some blacks use phrases such as "He be goin to the store." Does that mean that they speak a separate Black English or "Ebonics?" Many blacks think they do. They claim this is part of a special and distinct cultural carryover from the African past. They take pride in it. But is there really such a thing as Black English? Why do some blacks defend it so vigorously? Does their advocacy of it as a teaching approach or learning model help or hurt black students? If whites insisted that black students could not learn standard English without special language aids would blacks brand them as racists?

I was dumbstruck when I heard that the Oakland Board of Education in December 1996, voted to recognize "Black English" as a second language. I thought the debate over the use of "Black English" had pretty much died a merciful death years ago. At the height of the "black is beautiful" movement during the 1960s, it was fashionable for black militants to proudly boast that when blacks "talked black," the so-called language of the ghetto, they were rejecting the white man's culture, and rebelling against white authority.[1]

Many blacks who spoke the standard English were taunted for trying to "act white." Many black writers went through deft acrobatic circus loops in articles trying to defend the legitimacy of "Black English." Blacks were told that this way of speaking was a survival of their African past and they should take pride in it. During the 1980s, they redubbed "Black English" with a new name, Ebonics (ebony and phonics) declared it a separate language and demanded that educators recognize and include it in their school district's curriculum.[2]

The supporters of Ebonics are certainly right to criticize those teachers and school administrators that view black students who speak in an unconventional dialect as hopeless dunces who cannot be educated. This is condescension at best, and racism at worst. The humbug that blacks cannot learn like whites became a dim-witted self-fulfilling prophecy that put many black students at educational risk. The blacks that spoke this way were not dumber than whites. They simply picked up this pattern of speech in their home or from their peers on the streets.

However, the converts to and advocates of Ebonics still

relied on a dangerous stew of stereotypes and educational as well as cultural misassumptions about blacks. They erroneously believe that most blacks communicate in the same unconventional dialect. In its resolution, the Oakland School Board repeatedly called it "the predominantly primary language" of blacks. Some black leaders even made the ridiculous and stereotypical assertion that many blacks learn this kind of talk in the home and on the streets. Many do not. There is no such thing as uniform "black talk." Blacks, as do other ethnic groups, use the full range of tones, inflections, and accents in their speech depending on their education, family background, and the region where they live.

Some young blacks, heavily influenced by rap, hip-hop culture, slang, and street talk, mispronounce words, misplace verb tenses, or "code switch" when they talk to each other. Many young whites, Latinos, and Asians do the same. There is no conclusive proof that "Black English," as some blacks and linguists assert, has a separate syntax, grammar, and structure that fulfill all the requirements of a separate language.

Some black writers and educators have gone through more tortured gyrations trying to make the case that this type of speech is a cultural survival of African linguistic and speech patterns. All the African slaves did not come from the same region, belong to the same ethnic group, share the same culture, or speak the same language. There are more than 1,000 ethnic groups in the 52 nations on the African continent. They speak hundreds of languages, and there are thousands of regional dialects and linguistic influences. Long before

157

the European slavers began their systematic decimation of African populations, Arabic heavily influenced many of those languages and dialects. Despite this, some Ebonics advocates even make the absurd claim that 80 percent of blacks speak "Black English."[3]

The Oakland School Board went much further and proclaimed "black speak" a direct derivative of West and Central African language systems—Niger-Congo languages. It sounded plausible to some. The majority of black slaves in North America did come from West and Central Africa. Some linguists agree that the Niger-Congo languages were the languages spoken throughout the region. Other linguists and Africa experts, however, have repeatedly pointed out that this is not a unitary language but a widely differentiated grouping of languages that have evolved so distinctly apart over thousands of years that many of the words, meanings, and sounds within this language grouping are totally different from each other.[4]

Even if it was one language, four hundred years of black acculturation in America has effectively washed out most traces of African linguistic patterns and cultural traditions. The Oakland School Board and Ebonics advocates ignored all this. They gave conflicting and muddled definitions of what they consider "Black English" and completely disregarded the class background and educational deficiencies that more likely explain why some blacks say: "He <u>be</u> going to the store," rather than, "He is going to the store."[5]

Ebonics advocates make the dubious claim that devising new teaching methods based on Ebonics will help black students learn standard English easier. The Oakland School Board zoomed to the outer limits of inaneness by claiming that black students were doomed to fail in school unless they were "instructed" in English and their primary language (i.e., Ebonics). It even made the fantastic boast that an Ebonics program would instantly "remedy" the supposedly chronic below standard test scores of black students in English.

Before the mass outcry forced the Oakland school officials within days to back peddle fast from their original line, they were apparently prepared to squander time and pirate money from other underfunded programs in a desperate attempt to prove that their learning theory works.

There is absolutely no evidence to support any of this. The Ebonics advocates base their shaky case on patchy and inconclusive studies on other language groups, mainly those who speak Spanish and Chinese. For several years the Los Angeles Unified School District has had a program of "special language" instruction for black and non-white students. Beyond a few anecdotal success stories, teachers and administrators have produced no measured evidence that this program has boosted the student's verbal achievement.

This points to one of the most gaping instances of sightlessness of the Ebonic advocates. They presume that blacks are chronic educational failures. They are not. Over eighty percent of blacks graduated from high school and nearly thirty-five percent were enrolled in college in 1996. In 1994, four young African-American males were awarded Rhodes Scholarships, and 300, 000 young black high schoolers competed nationwide in the annual NAACP Academic, Cultural, Technological and Scientific Olympics (ACT-SO) competition. In 1995 and 1996, more African-Americans grabbed the Rhodes honors.[6]

The Ebonics advocates also do not explain how generations of black students, like white students, mastered standard English without their teachers approaching the subject as a foreign or incomprehensible language. The answer is simple. These students were taught by teachers who were dedicated and determined that they excel in their studies. They held black students to the same educational standards and accountability as whites and in many cases they got solid results.

In spite of the voguish claim that black students fail because standard English is supposedly so alien to them, educators who have devised these programs during the 1980s and 1990s have proven this is a fraud: The Accelerated Schools Program, The Comer School Development Program, the Higher Order Thinking Skills Program, The IBM Writing to Read Program, The National Urban Alliance's Cognition and Comprehensive Program, Reading Recovery, The School-Based Instructional Leadership Program, and Success for All.[7]

These programs have had modest to spectacular success in raising the reading and achievement level of many black students. Their approaches are different but they have several things in common. They challenge students to learn, set specific goals, demand active participation of the students (and in most cases the parents), emphasize clarity of assignments, give positive and constant direction to the students, and continually monitor their progress.

The cruel irony is that if a white group had called blacks educational defectives and demanded that they be stacked in special programs because they cannot learn or speak standard English, they would be loudly denounced as racists. Yet whites did not make that demand. Blacks did, and they must bear a small part of the blame for hardening the suspicions of many whites that blacks are mentally inferior or social misfits who need costly and time consuming special aids, texts, training, and remedial programs to learn. This could make even more employers believe that blacks are unstable, uncooperative, dishonest, uneducated, crime-prone, and not fit to be hired.

The Ebonics advocates certainly cannot be incriminated for the social and educational plight of many African-Americans. This happened long before they came along. That is what made the debate over Ebonics even more heartbreaking.

A Final Comment: Black leaders, educators, and parents should demand quality education and greater funding for teacher training programs. They should insist that teachers and school administrators recognize, accept, and respect cultural diversity among students, and adhere to the highest educational standards in predominantly minority school districts. To argue or imply that most, many, or even all, black students cannot master standard English without a radical racially divisive overhaul of the educational system is not only a slavish bow to fringe Afrocentrism and political correctness, it is a flat-out fallacy.

A happy note: on May 5, 1997, the Oakland school board finally came to its senses and approved a workable plan to improve the district's reading levels. It did not include Ebonics.[8]◆

16

The Continuing Crisis of the Negro Intellectual

During the 1960's black intellectuals railed against white academics for monoplizing and distorting published works on the black experience. They demanded that they be given the chance, to write, research, get funding for and have published scholarly works on the black struggle and black thought. Now that many have that chance, what have they done with it? Why are most of the major, scholarly books on the black experience still churned out by whites? Why are far too many of the books produced by black scholars shallow, pretentious, pop hits? Why are many black intellectuals more concerned with prosperity and celebrity status than making the hard effort to turn out works that will stand the test of time and are truly worthy of being called an "important work"?

I have always prided myself on my large collection of books by black authors. That is why I was surprised when a friend, after peering at the academic books in my library on contemporary American racial history, asked so few none of the books were written by blacks. The question seemed more like an accusation than a question. I quickly grabbed books by several black scholars and waved them in front of him as examples of solid, compelling works that enhance understanding of the issues and events of the black experience in America. My answer satisfied him. It did not satisfy me.

When he left, I sat for a long time staring at my bookshelf. I realized why he asked the question. Other than the handful of books I showed him, the majority of my books on racial issues were written by white authors. They are first-rate scholarly works, based on an exhaustive mix of primary and secondary sources, archives, private papers, government documents and reports, newspaper articles, and personal interviews. They were published by non-academic presses and were written in a non-pedantic, and highly readable style. These books are frequently referenced and discussed by students, academics, policy makers, and the general reading public. They will stand the test of time as important books.

I cannot say the same for the books by many black intellectuals. And it is irritating because I remember during the 1960s black militants savagely attacked white academics for carving out a lucrative cottage industry "studying" blacks. They charged that white academics had easy access to research and foundation grants, paid sabbaticals, an unlimited supply of eager students to comb the archives for source material, and unlimited use of libraries. Their ultimate pay-off was a fat contract from a mainstream publisher.

Black activists demanded that colleges and universities hire and promote more blacks to faculty positions, provide them equal time and money for research, and for publishers to provide them with contracts. Once this happened it was expected that black scholars would trigger an avalanche of solidly researched books on the black struggle.

The critics were right and wrong. In that era, white academics had a total lock on campus resources and a wide open path to the publishing world. Many editors did not believe that blacks were capable of serious scholarship. That has changed. There are many respected black scholars on dozens of college campuses. Many have tenured positions, have access to libraries, can secure grants, and have an ample supply of student researchers. Mainstream publishers publish more books by blacks than ever. The critics were wrong in expecting all black scholars to publish books that pass rigorous intellectual muster. They are still far and away too few.

Many of the books by black authors published by mainstream publishers fall into these predictable categories: crime and violence, health, finance, family breakdown, male-female relationships, poverty, evil black conservatives, popular (mostly rap)

165

culture, and spirituality. Nearly all are thin volumes of the author's recycled essays or newspaper articles. The writers offer little or no documentation, reference notes, or a bibliography to support their opinions. The only unifying theme of their book is "racial matters." Most of these books smack of crass intellectual masturbation hastily tossed together. The abysmal failure of far too many black intellectuals to produce top line scholarly works painfully betrays the hard fight to recapture black history from the white academics whom they claim monopolized and distorted the black experience.

In trying to figure out why many have failed to produce quality works, I thought of the devastating and bitter assault writer Harold Cruse made on black intellectuals in his *The Crisis of the Negro Intellectual* a quarter century ago. Cruse raked black scholars and activists over the coals for being hopelessly trapped in the ideological hip-pocket of white liberals and leftists, and not thinking and acting for themselves.

It is not necessary to bait black intellectuals or grind ideological axes as Cruse did. I must ask is their failure due to intellectual laziness? Do major publishers encourage black writers to write shallow, pretentious works in order to make fast sales? Do black readers fawn over these authors because they demand less, and accept less, from black writers? Do reviewers make a doltish bow to political and racial correctness by hailing the works of these intellectual impostors as deeply profound probes of racial problems?

It is all of the above. Many black intellectuals have figured out that the key to publishing success is not in spending years enduring and endeavoring on research and interviews, hassling with students, going through countless circus loops to get research grants, and having their works subjected to unsparing criticism from other academics. Instead, some can reap instant success pontificating on racism on TV talk shows, collecting steep honorariums for spewing their pop social theories at colleges, and hobnobbing with the social elites on the banquet circuit.

◆ ◆ ◆ ◆ ◆

I would like to think that a new crop of black scholars will mine the rich lode of historical material on the black experience and produce works of scholarship worthy of the name. I am not optimistic. Weaned on sound-bites, photo-opportunities, and tabloid journalism, nurtured on MTV videos, spoon fed information via the Internet, many young people have made instant gratification a fetish, and reading books and newspapers a dead art. The dumbing down of black America almost certainly will worsen. And the up-and-coming black intellectuals will likely take the cue and realize that the quick and dirty way to recognition is to churn out an instant "hit."

Meanwhile those black writers that truly hold upright the torch of scholarship will continue to be lonely souls turning out first-rate works that expand our awareness of the contemporary historical black experience. This is a pity. Black scholars can do much better and black readers deserve much better.

167

A Final Comment: How can we get more black scholars and intellectuals to write scholarly works truly worthy of the name? It is a two-way street. Those scholars who are willing to take the time must make the effort to produce a solid piece of work on some aspect of the historical experience that contains lessons that can be applied to the present. Black scholars will take the time and make the effort *if* they feel there is an audience for their work. This will mean that more publishers must publish and promote these works and more of the reading public must buy them. When this happens more black scholars and intellectuals will measure the value of their work by the posterity as well as the prosperity it brings them.◆

Black Men, White Women, Black Obsession

There are few things that make many black women and men angrier that the notion of black men dating, marrying, and having sexual relations with white women. What makes this such a hot button issue? Why do so many blacks ignore the fact that the vast majority of black men date and marry black women? Why do so many blacks continue to believe that most prominent black men are married to white women? What does the issue of who someone chooses to date or marry have to do with the crisis issues of racism, poverty, drugs, and violence that plague many black communities? Why have so many blacks self-appointed themselves as the interracial sexual watchdogs of black America?

I shuddered when I was asked to participate in a panel discussion that was billed as a "soul search" on black male-female relationships. In the past, these kinds of panels have turned into worthless, no worse, destructive gripe sessions. This time was no different. The panel's facilitator slowly ticked off the favorite complaints of black men and women against each other. They are: insensitive, abusive, derelict, and irresponsible. Many in the audience vigorously nodded their heads in agreement. When the facilitator paused and slyly said, "how about black men chasing white women," the roar from the audience was thundering.

The popular line goes likes this: when a black man gets money he runs out and marries a white woman. Athletes, entertainers, musicians, politicians, and prominent professionals are supposedly the most horrid offenders. The notion that black men are in an incessant carnal hunt for white women is the centerpiece of books, records, and a popular movie. It has sparked near universal black rage and condemnation.

The O.J. Simpson case proved that with a vengeance. While many African-Americans publicly stated that they thought he was innocent, privately they blasted him for marrying a white woman. Shortly after he was arrested for the murders of his ex-wife, Nicole Brown Simpson and Ron Goldman, a *Washington Post* columnist asked several black women in beauty shops and on the streets what they thought of O.J. and Nicole. Four out of five women were pitiless. They generally felt, as one put it, "That's what O.J.

gets for being with a white woman."[1]

The hysteria of many blacks over interracial marriage is wrong-headed, and a foolish waste of time and energy that could be used to pursue solutions to the problem of racially-motivated violence, the drug plague, gang violence, the slash and burn of education and social services, the soaring criminalizing of and imprisonment rate of black men and women, the obliteration of affirmative action, and black family destabilization.

These are the crisis problems and needs that profoundly threaten many blacks. These are not chic or fun things to talk about. They do not allow black men and women to vent, blame, scapegoat, and point fingers at each other.

Even with the rise in the number of interracial marriages over the past two decades, the numbers of black men and white women who marry each other are barely a blip on the marriage chart and not much more than that on the interracial marriage chart. In 1994, of the 1.3 million interracial marriages in America, about 200,000 were between black men and white women. The same year, 98 percent of black men that married picked black, not white (or other non-black women), women as their spouses.[2]

◆ ◆ ◆ ◆ ◆

This argument is meaningless to many blacks. They have long resented interracial marriages. Before the Supreme Court in 1967 struck down all state bans against interracial marriage, surveys showed that almost as many blacks as whites

171

frowned on black and white marriages. The ambivalence remains. A National Opinion Research Center poll in 1991 found that two-thirds of blacks neither "favored nor opposed" interracial marriage.

Although anti-miscegenation laws were brutal racial exclusionary measures designed to reinforce black inferiority, the poll revealed that nearly one in ten blacks still thought interracial marriage should be illegal.

Some blacks justify their brand of interracial marriage exclusion by saying that they are not bigots, but simply concerned with shielding their sons and daughters from the agony and hostility of an unforgiving and unyielding white society. They claim that children of interracial marriages will suffer mightily from taunts and rejection by whites (and some blacks). There is some merit to this argument. Some interracial couples and their children do suffer insults and rejection. Many others, of course, do not. But even if their lives were a bed of societal thorns, this is not the argument or expressed concern that drives black opponents of interracial marriage. The greater number fall back on the stock and near ritual retort that black men have no business with white or non-black women, and those who are with them are "race traitors."

In an informal poll taken three years after the 1991 National Opinion Research Center's poll, little had changed: forty percent of black women and a significant percentage of black men said they would not date a person of another race. Few bothered to give any reasons why.[3]

172

However, many blacks who play hard ball on the issue of interracial marriage take it as an article of faith that black men are obsessed with European beauty standards and that white women are trophies that fulfill black men's desire for power, status, and acceptance in the white world. These men supposedly think black women are poor imitations of white women and tolerate them as necessary evils.

This is a variation on the old theme that black men who date or marry white women have a terminal identity crisis resulting in low self-esteem and are using these women to escape from their own characteristic "blackness." They are the prototypic marginal man, rejected by a hostile white world and seeking escape from an insecure and fearful black world. This allegedly self-hate-filled black man can never belong to either. There is no end to the reasons given to explain the aberrant sexual behavior of a black man and a white woman who mate. They are supposedly: rebelling against authority; repudiating society's norms and values; answering the call of the jungle wild; or infatuated with the sexual exotica of each other.

Much of this boils down mostly to opinion, gossip, anecdote, rumor, envy, jealousy, and ignorance. Researchers find no evidence that black men and white women who date or marry are psychologically impaired. They find that the degree of personal and professional compatibility between them often matches or exceeds that of black couples.

The separation/divorce rate for black male-white female couples is only marginally less than black couples. Black and white marriages generally last as long and are as stable as the marriages of couples of the same race. Mixed couples have to have stronger personalities, character, and more self-assurance to withstand the stares, harassment, and hostility from many blacks and whites. [4]

◆ ◆ ◆ ◆ ◆

Black women are not losing their men to white women, they are losing them to the growing gender gorge that has badly shrunk the pool of marriageable black men. In 1992, there were 815,000 black women in "white collar" professions compared to 564,000 black men. Black women had increased their numbers sixty-four percent in corporate management positions; black men only twenty-two percent. In 1982, there were 1.2 black female professionals for every black male professional.

A decade later the ratio of black female professionals to black male professionals had widened to almost double that of black men. By 1994, there were more black women than men in major corporations, and for the first time in U.S. history, black single female heads of households earned as much as their white female counterparts.[5]

More black females than black males were graduating from high school. Fourteen percent of black women had college degrees compared to twelve percent of black men. The high rate of unemployment, murder, drug use, and chronic disease among black men has made more black women cynical about their ability to find a suitable mate. The one out of three young black men in jail, on probation, or parole who have been forced to trade a college degree for a jail cell has further increased the gender isolation and despair of many black women[6]

The fear of prominent, educated black men or even media created embarrassments such as basketballer Dennis Rodman, or media created bad boys such as Clarence Thomas and O.J. en masse marrying white women of any income or education group is an equally false fear. For every one of them that many blacks logotype as racial traitors for marrying white women, there are dozens of other black male celebrities or public figures such as Magic Johnson, Michael Jordan, Eddie Murphy, Bill Cosby, Denzel Washington, Spike Lee, Colin Powell, Andrew Young, John H. Johnson, and Mike Tyson who married black women.

Some of the black men who do marry white women, and there are more of them than a decade ago, may be motivated by sexual idolatry, but most are not. They simply have more opportunities to meet and interact with whites at colleges, in the workplace, and at social settings. Love and marriage cannot be regulated by an artificial standard of emotional or racial correctness.

That is why the comparitively few black men who date or marry white women are not guilty of racial treason. But the many blacks who think they are are the ones who are guilty of a racial obsession.

A Final Comment: The cure is to be honest and recognize that most black men will date, marry, raise families, grow old and die with black women. For the relatively few black men who chose not to, it is nobody's business but their own. The vital problems that confront many African-Americans that demand change, and can be changed, require the full focus and energies of black men and women. One of them is not the issue of black men and white women.◆

18

Overcoming the Crisis in Black and Black

The crisis in black and black is profound and troubling. It has confused and jaded some blacks. It has caused despair among others. It has triggered hostility and conflict between still others. Is there a solution? Should the question even be asked that way? Or is it more important and productive for blacks to suggest workable, manageable strategies to overcome the crisis in black and black?

I can always count on someone asking the question, "What's the solution to our problems?" This is the question that African-Americans ask more frequently than any other. I always caution that the question is as absurd as is the attempt to answer it. There is not and cannot be any one solution to the 400-year-old American racial conflict that is tightly entangled in a complex web of social, cultural, economic, and political issues that are as old and as puzzling as time. The root of the black-white conflict lay in the need of America's corporate and political elite to preserve and expand its power, profit, and control. The best that I or anyone can do is suggest a few strategies and tactics for change that might work.

This first entails getting rid of the faddish idea of who is a leader and what constitutes a program. The whimsy that sprouted in the post 1960s civil rights meltdown, and helped generously along by the star- and tabloid-struck media of the 1990s, was that any black who had a loud voice, TV camera charisma, and could get whites infuriated at them was a leader. Many blacks confused media popularity with leadership. They forgot that leadership is earned. It could be earned by anyone who is positive and productive in whatever they do, makes a solid contribution to the enrichment of their community, and influences others to do the same. This could be anyone—a parent, tradesperson, professional, businessperson, artist, or a scholar—anyone.

I understand why many blacks ask the question. They are in a headlong search to find a way out of their crisis. They are tired of listening to some blacks shout racism to excuse black crime and fabricate fantastic tales of conspiracies to explain all black ills. They are tired of propping up celebrities and sports icons as leaders and role models. They know that when they fall from grace, much of America, and that includes many blacks too, swiftly and brutally turn on them.

They are fed up with the name calling and bashing by blacks in a servile sidewalk scrape to black political correctness of other blacks who think and act differently than them. They have little patience with those who reach back millenniums in the past and invent a feel-good history that ignores the proud history of black struggle and accomplishment in America.

They are stumped by those who turn black separateness into a linguistic fashion statement by pretending that blacks cannot speak or learn English without special props. They are bitterly disappointed that the radiant warmth of the Million Man March quickly turned to desolate cold. They wonder if some blacks get their kicks off bashing gays because they are the softest of soft targets, and are hated almost as much as blacks are by many bigoted Americans.

They are enraged that some black rappers, filmmakers, and writers financially gorge themselves by making the world believe that the ghetto experience is every black's experience. They are concerned that some black intellectuals seek anointment as Negro experts on TV shows, churn out shallow books on race, and collect massive honorariums rather than producing quality works on contemporary history. All the while they ask, "Where are the black leaders that once fought the tough fights against poverty and racism?"

The crisis in black and white of a quarter century ago has today turned into the even more murky and potentially dangerous internal crisis and conflict between and among African-Americans. This not only raises the Mt. Everest size problems that face many blacks even higher, but the crisis within makes them harder to combat.

One example is enough to make the point. When the California Commission on the Status of African-American Males in March 1997 issued a report on the dreary plight of many young black males, a friend shrugged and quipped that it is more of the same old story. She was right.

The Commission's report was a virtual carbon copy of the report it issued four years earlier. It found then and now that black males in California have a shorter life expectancy, fewer educational opportunities, higher levels of unemployment and poverty, lower income, and much higher incarceration rates than whites. Although it was California, the same report could have been issued in any other state in the Union with a significant black population.[1]

Here we had yet another report from a government commission on the "endangered black male," or worse that told how blacks are on the verge of extinction. It was frustrating for me to read this because I know that private industry, government policy makers, and much of the public will do little about it. They can and should be blamed for the scrap heap of false or broken promises, indifference, or flat-out hostility toward blacks. But how can an effective battle be waged for the timeless laundry list of needs that include: more funding for jobs, health, education, social services, child care, drug and treatment programs, criminal justice and non-punitive welfare reform, with some in the army going in one direction, some in another, while some raise the white flag of surrender?

◆ ◆ ◆ ◆ ◆

The answer is that there cannot, will not, or maybe even should not, be complete agreement by blacks on a unified battle plan to attack racial problems. There can be agreement by many black professional, business persons, and workers to try and make what works work even better. There is much talk about the supposed $400 billion dollars that blacks spend on goods and services in America and what would happen if those dollars were made to work for them.[2]

This makes good parlor conversation, trendy debate, and interesting reading in articles, and books. But the majority of blacks, like whites, and other non-blacks, are workers and consumers, not owners and producers. It has always been that way and in the American capitalistic structure, it will always be that way. The black working and middle class does field big numbers, are highly educated, and possess skills and economic clout like never before. They are the role models of success and achievement that young black males and females frantically need to interact with.

This is vastly important because the crisis has had its most deadly consequences for many young African-Americans. The level of black-on-black slaughter is still ridiculously high. The killings of rappers Notorious B.I.G. and Tupac Shakur

181

were perhaps the harshest reminder that many young black males are still at mortal risk from homicide.

The stop the violence movement initiated by some young blacks during the mid-1990s made more blacks not only aware of the disproportionate high levels of violence within some black communities but also the physical abuse of African-American children in many black homes. Some dedicated black social workers, psychologists and health professionals nationally have begun programs to mediate and counsel parents in anti-violence prevention techniques, and train African-American volunteer "child advocates" in child counseling.

This is also a reminder that haranguing the "white media" for perpetuating negative images flies wide of the mark. The better course is for blacks to stop assassinating their own image in word and deed. They can start by putting the overwhelming majority of young blacks who achieve on a pedestal. Black-owned radio stations should routinely interview them. Black-owned newspapers should regularly do profiles and features on them. Black organizations and political leaders should continually honor them.

Meanwhile, a growing number of black parents and professionals have answered the challenge. The 100 Black Men organization nationally sponsors mentoring programs and provides scholarships and grants to young blacks. There have been a series of "black male crisis" conferences nationally during the 1990s in which black professionals and businesspersons shared their experiences with hundreds of high school and junior high school students. The Million Man March in October 1995, despite its mountainous flaws and badly missed opportunities, was still a solid example of what all classes of blacks can do when they are aroused. With the wrinkles ironed out, it remains a useful model for future local community organizing.

Many black educators, businesspersons, and professionals periodically sponsor conferences in which they provide parents with learning tips and materials to help them improve the study habits of their children. They reject the idea that black students cannot learn standard English or cannot learn anything without gimmicks. Their efforts also point to the even greater need for black professionals and educators to create self-help programs that provide educational scholarships, career counseling, and job and skills training programs to break the mesmerizing Air Jordan sports effect and recycle those young blacks who are sports junkies into serious students.

Black parents, whose sons or daughters are involved in athletic programs, can do their duty and hold coaches, teachers and school administrators accountable for their children's courses, grades and campus activities. If their sons or daughters do not perform in the classroom, they should not get to perform on the field or the court.

More parents and educators are realizing that Super Bowls, NBA championships, and Master's Tournaments provide fame and fortune to football players such as Deion Sanders, basketball players such as Michael Jordan, and golfers such as a Tiger Woods. For countless others they provide only delusions.

♦ ♦ ♦ ♦ ♦

The work of some black professionals and parents is paying off. The overwhelming majority of young blacks graduated from high school in 1996, and have drop-out rates no greater than whites. They now appear less likely to use drugs and alcohol than young whites, and most unemployed young blacks continue to actively search for jobs.

This still is not enough. There are too many blacks who have fallen, or are in danger of falling victim to the streets. They must be given hope. The most urgent need is to focus on job and skills training. More black professionals, businesspersons, and workers can organize or conduct bi-weekly or monthly training workshops that emphasize math, science, data processing, computer programming, reading, and writing skills. The workshops could offer pointers on proper grooming, dress, manners as well as instruction in how to properly conduct a job search, fill out an application and how to handle interviews.

Black entrepreneurs can train and counsel young blacks in business management, marketing, leasing, franchising, financial planning, and investments. African-American churches, neighborhood centers, service agencies, and businesses can donate facilities, reading materials and equipment for business preparation, job skills development, and counseling workshops. They can also push hard to get more blacks supplied with computers, trained in how to use them, and how to develop a complete mastery of the information superhighway.

This is still not enough. Here are a few more actions that could be done:

• Support black businesses that offer quality service and products at competitive prices and that pledge to invest a percentage of their profits in, or create, social and educational programs in the black communities. The so-called economic success miracle of Latinos and Asians, much marveled at by blacks and whites, is really no miracle. They create and patronize their own businesses because they know that there is a social dividend in it for them. That is their dollars will be automatically "recycled" into scholarship, recreation, mentoring, skills training, and business development programs within their communities.

• Applaud and support the athletes and entertainers who volunteer their time and money to support camps, foundations, scholarship programs, and other activities for the young and poor. Do not assume that all prominent and celebrity-name blacks do nothing. Many make their contributions behind the scenes and away from the glare of publicity.

• Discourage young (and not so young) blacks from buying records, tapes and videos, tickets to plays and movies, and spending brain-deadening hours cackling at sit-coms that turn them into spectacles of degradation. Encourage them to spend money and support anything and everything uplifting from positive Rap to clean comedy that enhances black success and achievement.

• Write letters, send e-mails, faxes, telephone calls to black and non-black Hollywood producers, newspaper editors, TV and radio producers, demanding more accurate and honest news, depictions, and portrayals of black life. Patronize or invest in film projects by independent black filmmakers who make documentaries and films (e.g., the films *Once Upon A Time When We Were Colored* in 1996 and *Soul Food* in 1997) that both entertain and inspired.

• Encourage tolerance, not name calling, among blacks with political and gender differences. The Million Man March demonstrated that there are enough common problems and opportunities for everyone from black gays to conservatives to agree and work on together.

• Teach and take pride in black history which is American history.

• Be a leader by positive example no matter what your area of interest or work.

These actions are not as appealing as spouting grandiose theories of global white supremacy. They are not as sexy or enticing as black male or female bashing. They will not make anyone an instant leader. They will not grab a spot on the *Oprah Show*. They will require time and work. They will be appreciated by only a few. But they are important steps toward recognizing and overcoming the crisis in black and black.

A Final Comment: No, a caveat. This is not *the* answer or *the* blueprint for change. It is only my thoughts about strategies that are working and that can work even better.◆

Our Stockholm
Syndrome—A Postscript

It is heresy to say it among some blacks, but it is true.
African-Americans are in their tastes, views, and ad-
herence to tradition more American than white Americans. This should not surprise when one considers
what blacks have made of America and what America
has made of them. This process of identification with
the best and worst of America is similar to the psycho/
social condition (malady) called the Stockholm Syndrome. What is the syndrome? How does it apply to
blacks? Why are blacks more American than white
Americans? Why do so many blacks persist in thinking that they are different or deny that they are different than whites?

I immediately contacted my publisher Middle Passage Press, a small black-owned company, when the
first version of my book *The Assassination of the Black Male*

Image was published in 1994. I asked them to send a review copy of the book to a black columnist whom I had known and respected for some time. For many years he has written a regular, and very popular column for one of America's leading newspapers. He sees himself as a militant, no nonsense guy when it comes to taking tough stands on the hard racial issues. I knew from our prior conversations that he also admired and was very interested in my writings.

My publisher quickly sent him a copy for review. I fully expected that he would give the book at least a mention in his column. When a few weeks passed without hearing anything, the publisher dutifully followed up to make sure that he had received the book. He had. He indicated that he liked it and would eventually do something on it. He never did.

Two years later, in 1996, Simon & Schuster published a new and revised version of the same book. A week after it came out I got an excited call from the writer/acquaintance. He said that he had just gotten off the phone talking with the publicity director for Simon & Schuster and that he very much wanted to do a full column on me and the book.

As we talked, he suddenly, paused in mid-sentence, and said, "You know I've had the older version of your book all these years and I never did anything with it. And here I get one call from this young white woman, with the sweet, soft voice from Simon & Schuster, and I rush to call you for an interview." I did not respond nor was I surprised, or offended by his racial epiphany. His slight was not malicious, deliberate, or intentional.

He was no different than many other blacks who identify with and respond to the real power of a prestigious mainstream New York publishing giant, while ignoring a small black publisher. When they call you respond or at least acknowledge them. They represented two different worlds. To him one represented status, power, and most importantly validation by the white world. The other, well. . . .

◆ ◆ ◆ ◆ ◆

My acquaintance is not a hypocrite; and he is not alone. The examples are bottomless. A prestigious national black professional association which considers itself single-mindedly committed to the fight to promote racial justice and end employment discrimination listed the following names as "invited speakers" at its national convention in 1997:

President Bill Clinton
Kofi Annan
Oprah Winfrey
Colin Powell
Michael Jordan
Dennis Rodman
Alexis Herman
J.C. Watts

Was this group serious? The chances were slim to none that all, most, or perhaps any of these individuals would show yet they listed them anyway because they represented status, power, and validation by the white world.

191

I checked the covers and lead feature stories of the major national black magazines for six months in 1996 and in 1997 and with one exception, they were all features on the biggest name black celebrities in sports or entertainment, nearly all of whom had graced their covers numerous times in the past. Yes, it is true that white popular magazines do the same. And that is the point. Black publications did the same because star power represented status, power, and validation by the white world.

This is not cheap shot criticism. I mention it only to point out yet another perplexity that blacks face in America.

African-Americans remind me of the bank personnel and customers who were taken hostage by a band of robbers during a bank robbery in Stockholm, Sweden in the 1970's. During the tense stand-off, police and city officials were struck dumb at how the hostages in the bank displayed these characteristics: (a) positive feelings toward the crooks; (b) their positive feelings were reciprocated by the crooks toward the captives; and (c) negative feelings toward police and officials. In their dire state of confusion, fear, dependency, and need, the good guys and bad guys were blurred and then reversed in the minds of the hostages. They identified with their captors.

Psychologists had a field day with this one. They had discovered a new psychological malady. They promptly labeled this condition the "Stockholm Syndrome." Since then when any individual or group identifies with a dominant power no matter how perverted, perverse, and harmful to them they are said to suffer from this condition. African-Americans in the context of America are not hostages, captives, or victims. And America is not a criminal. But, many African-Americans do exhibit similar tendencies as the Stockholm bank hostages. Their captor is American values.

Some disagree and claim that this bizarre condition strikes only black conservatives, celebrities, politicians, and assorted public figures who are praised, pampered, and enriched by the "white establishment" and will do anything to identify with and cater to it. These individuals are soft and easy targets to revile.[1]

The truth is that *all* blacks have had to do much to survive America. Despite four centuries of slavery, segregation, discrimination, violence, and brutality. No matter how much blacks protest it, deny it, and try to delude themselves about it, they hungrily identify with the dominant standards and values of America—the best and worst of America. They have no choice. America is their only frame of reference.

Some have tried to shed the syndrome by claiming that they are African people. They wear African garb, adopt African names, take trips to Africa, learn a few words of an African language, and send their children to all-black schools. Some call themselves Pan-Africanists. Some denounce whites as devils. Some renounce voting and pride themselves on not taking part in America's political process.

Still, the signs are everywhere that most, if not all, African-Americans are trapped by America. They go to work, own a business or a profession or trade, attend school, shop in the same stores, read the same magazines, newspapers, listen to the same radio shows, and watch the same TV programs, pay the same taxes, and many drive the same late model cars that white Americans do. They do everything and sometimes much more than white Americans do to display their emersion in American values. No matter how hard they try, sooner or later, the stark realization hits many that their standards and values are the same as America's standards and values.

Along the way many African-Americans sometimes deliberately, but more likely subliminally, measure the worth of all African-Americans by those standards. The closer an African-American comes to them, the more acceptable they become to other African-Americans.

This is not a negative judgment, nor a put down. I, and nearly every other African-American, have at times been guilty of applying the yardstick of American values to those we like, love, dislike, hate, or ignore in work, business, school, or play to those whom we consider successful and those whom we dismiss as failures, to those whom we look up to, and those whom we look down on. That we apply the yardstick of America's values to them is not necessarily a bad thing. What is bad is that we have to do it. What is worse is that we deny that we do it.

A century ago, black scholar W.E.B. Dubois dissected the eternal turmoil and confusion in the black psyche in *The Souls of Black Folks,* "One ever feels his two-ness, an American, a

Negro: two souls, two thoughts, two unreconciled strivings, two warring ideals in one dark body, whose dogged strength alone keeps it from being torn asunder."[2]

Those two warring ideals have claimed many victims, scuttled many hopes, and fostered many phantasms among African-Americans, but it also has created many opportunities, fulfilled many hopes, and enriched many African-Americans. As long as blacks are torn by those two warring ideals there will always be more hope than despair that many may discover a way out of the crisis in black and black.

A Final Comment: Even the bank captives in Sweden found a way out. They eventually snapped back to reality and their testimony helped put the bank robbers behind bars.◆

References

Our Own Worst Enemy—An Overview

1. Charles Silberman, *The Crisis in Black and White* (New York: Random House, 1964).

1
I Believe in America: Understanding a Clarence Thomas

1. *Washington Post*, February 27, 1997, 12.

2. W.E. B. DuBois, *The Philadelphia Negro* (1899, Reprint New York: Schocken Books, 1967) 37.

3. *USA Today*, July 29, 1991, 1.

4. *Christian Science Monitor*, April 18, 1995, 1; *U.S. News & World Report*, November 4, 1996, 28-30.

5. *Time*, February 28, 1994, 22; *Los Angeles Times*, May 16, 1997, 20.

6. John Hope Franklin, *From Slavery to Freedom* (New York: Random House, 1967) 573-607.

7. Frederick Douglass, "What are the Colored People Doing for Themselves?" in Howard Brotz (ed.) *Negro Social and Political Thought*, 1850-1920 (New York: Basic Books, 1966) 203-208.

8. Elliot Rudwick and August Meier, *From Plantation to Ghetto* (Hill and Wang, 1970).

9. Earl Ofari Hutchinson, *Blacks and Reds: Race and Class in Conflict, 1919-1990* (East Lansing, MI: Michigan State University Press, 1995) 112-114.

10. George Schuyler, *Black and Conservative* (New Rochelle, NY: Arlington House, 1966).

11. W.E. B. DuBois, *Crisis Magazine*, "Close Ranks," #16, July, 1918, 164-165.

12. "The Founding Program of the OAAU," in George Breitman, *By Any Means Necessary* (New York: Pathfinder Press, 1970) 33-67.

13. David Savage, "In the Matter of Justice Thomas," *Los*

Angeles Times Magazine, October 9, 1994, 20-25.

14. *Washington Post*, March 14, 1997, 27.

15. Chuck Stone, "The National Conference on Black Power," in Floyd D. Barbour, *The Black Power Revolt* (Boston: Porter Sargeant, 1968) 189-199; Marshall Frady, *Jesse: The Life and Pilgrimage of Jesse Jackson* (New York: Random House, 1996).

16. George E. Curry, "After the Million Man March," *Emerge*, February, 1996, 41; *Washington Post*, January 17, 1997, 9; *CSM*, September 16, 1996, 19.

17. *Black Enterprise*, March 1995, 24; Department of Commerce, Census Report, The Black Population in the United States, March 1994 and 1993"; *Black Enterprise*, June, 1997.

18. *Los Angeles Times*, November 6, 1996, 25.

19. *Washington Post*, April 21, 1996, 11.

20. Audrey Edwards, "Survey Report," *Black Enterprise*, August, 1990, 95; Jervis Anderson, "Black and Blue," *The New Yorker*, April 29-May 6, 1996, 64.

2
Rethinking the Million Man March

1. *New York Times*, October 16, 1996, B3.

2. Maize Woodford, *Black Scholar*, Fall, 1996, 35-40.

3. *Washington Post*, November 19, 1996, H5.

4. *Time*, September 23, 1996, 40; *Los Angeles Times*, April 23, 1997, B1.

5. Department of Commerce, Census Report, "The Black Population in the United States, March," 1993 and 1994.

6. *Newsweek*, October 30, 1995, 48.

7. *Wall Street Journal*, August 7, 1992, 4; William Oliver, "Sexual Conquest and Patterns of Black-on-Black Violence: A Statistical-Cultural Perspective," *Violence and Victims*, #4 (1989) 263-264; Reginald Stuart, "Behind Bars," *Emerge*, March, 1997, 44-48.

8. Scott Minnerbrook, "The Right Man for the Job?" *U.S. News & World Report*, October 16, 1995, 58-60.

9. *Washington Post*, December 8, 1996, C1.

3
The Air Jordan Effect

1. *Los Angeles Times*, September 9, 1995, C1.

2. *Los Angeles Times*, January 2, 1996, C1.

3. Arthur Ashe, *Days of Grace*, (New York: Knopf, 1993) 126.

4. John Simons, "Improbable Dreams," *U.S. News & World Report*, March 24, 1997, 51.

5. *Forbes*, December 16, 1996, 244; *Forbes*, December 18, 1995, 212.

6. Simons, "Improbable Dreams," 52.

7. Harry Edwards, "The Isolated Black Athlete," *Dollars & Sense*, May, 19, 1994, 26-30; *Los Angeles Times*, April 15, 1997, A1; *Los Angeles Times*, April 15, 1997, C4.

8. *Los Angeles Daily News*, April 27, 1997, C4.

9. Eleanor D. Branch, "Marketing the Games," *Black Enterprise*, July, 1995, 92.

10. Eric L. Smith, "Negotiating the Deals," *Black Enterprise*, July, 1995, 95.

11. Jim Naughton, *Chronicle of Higher Education*, July 26, 1996, 43-44.

12. *Washington Post*, August 14, 1994, 1.

13. Jimmie Briggs, "No Defense," *Emerge*, October, 1994, 52; Betsy Peoples, "Time Out," *Emerge*, October, 1996, 56-59.

14. Jack McCallum, "NCAA: A Sensible Proposition," January 20, 1997, 20.

15. *Los Angeles Times*, April 14, 1997, C1.

16. *People Weekly*, April 16, 1996, 60-62.

17. *Los Angeles Times*, April 22, 1997, C3; April 23, 1997, C3; April 29, 1997, C3.

18. Paul Newberry, *Associated Press*, April 14, 1997; Woods Interview, Oprah Winfrey Show, April 24, 1997.

4
Chasing Conspiracy Shadows

1. Gary Webb, "Dark Alliance," *San Jose Mercury News*, August, 18-20, 1996, 1.

2. Mary A. Mitchell, "Blacks and the Criminal Justice System," *Dollars & Sense* #28, 1996, 34-38.

3. *Christian Century*, December 11, 1996, 1221-1222.

4. Helen Cooper, "A Question of Justice: Do Prosecutors Target Minority Politicians?" *Wall Street Journal*, January 12, 1996, 1.

5. William F. Pepper, *Orders to Kill: The Truth Behind The Murder of Martin Luther King*, (Carrol & Graf, 1995).

6. Kenneth O'Reilly, *Racial Matters*, "The FBI's Secret File on Black America, 1960-1972" (New York: Free Press, 1989); Michael Friedly and David Gallen, *Martin Luther King-FBI File* (New York: Carrol & Graf, 1993).

7. William Shirer, *The Rise and Fall of the Third Reich* (New York: Ballantine Books, 1992).

8. Page Smith, *Democracy on Trial: The Japanese-American Evacuation and Relocation in World War II* (New York Simon and Schuster, 1995).

9. *Los Angeles Times*, April 18, 1996, 1; September 2, 1996, 5.

10. Richard Hofstadter, *The Paranoid Style in American Politics* (New York, Knopf, 1965).

5
"O.J. Is Guilty"

1. *Newsweek*, August 1, 1994, 20.

2. "Whites' Myths About Blacks," *U.S. News & World Report*, November 9, 1992, 47.

3. *Emerge*, October, 1996, 38-44.

6
The Five Dilemmas of Black Leaders

1. Robert Penn Warren, *Who Speaks for the Negro?* (New York: Random House, 1965).

2. *Los Angeles Times*, January 21, 1996, M5.

3. Amy Waldron, "The GOP's Shining Star," *Washington Monthly*, October, 1996, 34-40.

4. *Washington Post*, February 5, 1997, A16.

5. *Newsweek*, March 17, 1997, 60.

6. *Arizona Informant*, April 23, 1997, 17.

7
Farrakhan: The Ultimate Dilemma

1. *Newsweek*, October 30, 1995, 48.

2. Jervis Anderson, "Black and Blue," 64; *Los Angeles Times*, October 17, 1995, 11.

3. *Time*, February 28, 1994, 24-25.

4. *Wall Street Journal*, November 5, 1996, 23; October 30, 1996, 22.

5. *Washington Post*, March 14, 1997, 27; *Wall Street Journal*, March 6, 1997, 21.

8
My Gay Problem, Their Black Problem

1. Jervis Anderson, *Troubles I've Seen* (New York: Harper & Collins, 1997) 348.

2. Amy Abugo Ongini, *Black Nationalism, Black Masculinity and the Black Gay Cultural Imagination*, College Literature (March, 1997), 280-294;

3. *Jet*, January 10, 1994, 12; Gregory M. Herek and John Capitanio, "Black Heterosexuals: Attitudes Toward Lesbians and Gay Men in the United States," *Journal of Sex Research*, #32, 1995, 95-105.

4. Andrew Gillings, "On Interracial Dating," *Village Voice*, July 2, 1996, 31.

9
The Crisis in Black And Black

1. E. Franklin Frazier, *The Black Bourgeoisie* (New York: Macmillan Co., 1962) 108-109.

2. Derek T. Dingle, "Whatever Happened to Black Capitalism," *Black Enterprise*, August, 1990, 164, 162.

3. Maggie Jackson. "Equity Investment Fund for Minorities Slated," *AP Report*, May 8, 1997.

4. Department of Commerce, Census Report, "The Black Population in the United States," March, 1993 and 1994."

5. *Black Enterprise*, September, 1995, 22.

6. "Texaco: A Tarnished Star," *Emerge*, February, 1997, 36-40.

7. *Los Angeles Times*, March 16, 1997, 26; March 21, 1997, 1.

8. Danny R. Johnson, "Tobacco Stains," *Progressive*, December, 1992, 26-28.

9. *Black Enterprise*, March , 1997, 21.

10. Frazier, *The Black Bourgeoisie*, 181

10
Afrocentrism: Whose History to Believe?

1. Arnold Toynbee, *A Study of History* (New York: Oxford University Press, 1961).

2. Cheik Diop, *Civilization or Barbarism?* (Brooklyn: Lawrence Hill Books, 1991).

3. Robert Hughes, "The Fraying of America," *Time*, February 3, 1992, 44.

4. Mary Lefkowiticz, *Not Out of Africa*, (New York: Basic Books, 1996) 3.

5. Basil Davidson, *African Civilization Revisited: From Antiquity to Modern Times* (Trenton, N.J.:Africa World Press, 1991); W.E.B. DuBois, *The World and Africa* (New York: International Publishers, 1965).

6. J.D. Fage and Roland Oliver, eds., *Cambridge History of Africa* ,Vol. 1 (London: Cambridge, 1975).

7. Alex Boyd and Catherine Lenix Hooker, "Afro-Centrism: Hype or History," *Library Journal*, November 1, 1992, 46.

8. Molefi Kete Asante, *The Afrocentric Idea* (Philadelphia: Temple University Press, 1987) 159-181.

11
The Concrete Killing Fields

1. *Los Angeles Times*, April 23, 1997, B1

2. *Time*, September 23, 1996, 40.

3. *Washington Post*, November 19, 1995, H5.

4. *Los Angeles Times*, August 20, 1996, 15.

5. *Dallas Herald*, August 19, 1990, 10; Marjorie Zatz, "Racial, Ethnic Bias in Sentencing," 31, *Journal of Research in Crime and Delinquency*, 1987, 69-92.

6. Claude Brown, *Manchild in The Promised Land* (New York: New American Library, 1965) 312-313.

7. William Oliver, "Sexual Conquests and Pattern of Black-on-Black Violence," 263-264.

8. William Oliver, "Black Males and the Tough Guy Image: A Dysfunctional Compensatory Adaptation," *Western Journal of Black Studies* #8 (1984) 197-200.

9. Coramae Richey Mann, *Unequal Justice*, (Bloomington: Indiana University Press, 1993) 106.

10. Frantz Fanon, *The Wretched of the Earth* (New York: Grove Press, 1966) 248-249; Fanon, *A Dying Colonialism* (New York: Grove Press, 1967).

11. Douglas C. McDonald and Kenneth E. Carlson, *Sentencing in the Federal Courts: Does Race Matter?* (Washington D.C.: Department of Justice, December, 1993); Ronald Barri Flowers, *Minorities and Criminality* (New York: Greenwood Press, 1990).

12. National Commission on the Causes and Prevention of Violence, "Violence and the Media" (Washington D.C.: GPO, 1969, 251-252.

12
Hollywood's Booty Call

1. *Newsweek*, March 17, 1997, 58.

2. Johnnie L. Roberts, "Is Tinsletown Really Racist," *Newsweek*, March 18, 1996, 45.

3. National Urban League, *The State of Black America*, 1996, (NY: National Urban League, 1996) 213-231.

4. Roberts, "Is Tinsletown Really Racist," 44.

5. Phillip Foner, ed., *Paul Robeson Speaks* (New York: Bruner/ Mazel, 1978) 142, 520.

6. *New York Times*, May 28, 1995, E2.

7. *Los Angeles Times*, January 14, 1996, M3; February 6, 1996, E1.

8. *Los Angeles Times*, February 11, 1997, F1.

13
The Return of the Mau Mauer

14
Bad as I Wannabe

1. National Urban League, *State of Black America*, 1996, (NY: National Urban League, 1996) 213-231.

2. *BET Weekend*, May 1997, 4.

3. *Jet*, August 22, 1994, 21.

4. *Newsweek*, March 17, 1997, 62.

5. Paul Delaney, "Gangsta Rappers vs. The Mainstream Black Community," *USA Today*, January, 1995, 68-69.

6. Marc Spiegler, "Marketing Street Culture," *American Demographics*, November, 1996, 28-32.

15
The Fallacy of Talkin' Black

1. *Oakland Post*, December 12, 1996, 1.

2. Earl Ofari Hutchinson, "How 'Talking White' Spurred Ebonics," *San Francisco Chronicle*, December 30, 1996, 20.

3. John Iliffe, *Africans: The History of a Continent* (London: Cambridge University Press, 1995).

4. Roger Westcott, "African Languages and Prehistory" in Creighton Gabel and Norman R. Bennett, eds., *Reconstructing African Cultural History* (Boston: Boston University Press, 1967) 45-55; Roland Oliver & J.D. Fage, *A Short History of Africa* (New York: Facts on File, 1988) 17-18; "Should Black English Be Considered a Second Language," *Jet*, January 27, 1997, 12-16.

5. *Los Angeles Times*, December 20, 1996, 1; January 3, 1996, B1.

6. Glen Loury, "Blind Ignorance," *Emerge*, December, 1996-January, 1997, 65.

7. Daniel, "Instructional Approaches That Can Improve The Academic Performance of African-American Students," *Journal of Negro Education #63 (Winter 1994) 46-63.

8. *Los Angeles Times*, May 6, 1997, 1.

16
The Continuing Crisis of the Negro Intellectual]

17
Black Men, White Women, Black Obsession

1. *Washington Post*, June 24, 1994, D1.

2. *Jet*, June 3, 1996, 12-15.

3. *New York Times*, December 29, 1994, 4; *Ebony*, September, 1994, 42.

4. Ernest Porterfield, *Black and White Mixed Marriages* (Chicago: Nelson and Hall), 29; Andrew Billingsley, *Climbing Jacob's Ladder: The Enduring Legacy of African-American Families* (New York: Simon and Schuster, 1992) 247.

5. Sheryl Tucker Hilliard, "Black Women in Corporate America," *Black Enterprise*, August, 1994, 60; Department of Commerce, Census Report, Current Population Survey, March, 1995.

6. Department Commerce, Census Report. "The Black Population in The United States," March 1993 and 1994."

18
Overcoming the Crisis in Black and Black

1. *L.A. Watts Times*, March 1, 1997, 1.

2. Marjorie Whigham-Desir, "The Real Black Power," *Black Enterprise*, July, 1996, 60.

Our Stockholm Syndrome—A Postscript

1. T. Strentz, "The Stockholm Syndrome: Law Enforcement Policy and Hostage Behavior," in F.M. Ochberg and D.A. Soskis, ed., *Victims of Terrorism* (Boulder, Co.; Westview Press, 1982) 95-103; Barbara A. Huddleston-Mattai and P. Rudy Mattai, "The Sambo Mentality and the Stockholm Syndrome Revisited," *Journal of Black Studies*, Vol. 23, #3 (March, 1993) 344-357.

2. W.E.B. DuBois, *The Souls of Black Folks*, (1903 Reprint New York: Fawcett, 1964) 17.

Index